Another Pup?
The comprehensive guide to adding to or becoming a multi-dog household

Sarah Bartlett KCAI CD R QIDTI

DEDICATION

For Bella, Rosco, Rolo, Molly, Faith, and Jazz.
For my dogs past, present and future and for yours.

CONTENTS

ACKNOWLEDGMENTS

Thank you to Mark, my dog loving rock of a husband. Thanks to Celia & Gill for your help getting this book legible. Thank you to Isla for your support and input. Thanks to Alan for all of your support. Thank you to my dogs and other dogs that have taught me so much more than I can put into words.

1
Introduction

I currently have six dogs of my own, one being a youngster. Ripple (our cover girl) is under 12 months of age and is the reason I decided to write this book…introductions to the dogs will come later.

Before my current pack of 6, I have had four dogs of my own till their passing, one dog whom I inherited when I moved in with my husband who we later decided to rehome for her happiness and well-being, and countless foster dogs of varying breeds and ages. I used to offer a boarding service in my home for clients' dogs as part of my dog training and pet care business, so all of my dogs have had to deal with the constant change of pack structure and my levels of attention to them.

I am a qualified dog training instructor and specialise in multi-dog households, reactive/barky dogs, and puppy training. I'm a Kennel Club Accredited Instructor in companion dog training and KC Rally. QIDTI – qualified international dog training instructor. I have been professionally training dogs for eight years. My company which started off as pet care only was launched in 2007, and we have helped thousands of dogs over that time.
Apart from the various cross breeds I grew up with, I have had my own dogs since the age of 18 when I got my first house, and I have always had more than one dog.

I will be blunt in this book because having the wrong mix of dogs or being 'over dogged' leads to a very stressful and miserable life for you and the dogs.

This book is about getting a puppy in addition to the dogs you already have living with you, living in the house as part of the family.

Adding another dog to your household

What this book will help you with:

Adding another dog to your household when you already have one or more.

Primarily this book is aimed at adding a young puppy and not an adult dog, but if you are rescuing, for example, an older dog, it will undoubtedly help.

It will give you all the tools you need to prevent a 'doggy takeover' and prevent you from living with a gang of hooligans who take no notice of you.

It will advise on how to manage your existing dog or dogs including if they have behaviour issues or do things that wind you up…and stop your new dog from picking up on these things.

What it won't help you with:

Basic puppy training, there are plenty other books on the market who specialise in this…you will still need to train your puppy the basics!

It won't paint the ideal picture of perfectly behaved multi-dog households, because I honestly don't believe they exist. Having multiple dogs and preventing them from becoming a pack of wild dogs who you happen to live with and provide food for is hard work! The more you have, the harder work it is to get it right and keep it that way.

This book is not a substitute for calling in a professional when it is needed

Never, ever introduce more than one dog at a time, and certainly not two puppies at once.
Integrating two established packs (i.e. two dogs to another two dogs) is a whole other subject and deserves its own book, I have combined my three with my husband's two when I moved in with him, and though

the functional characters chapter will help with this, that is not the aim of this book.

I can promise you there will be some things in here that you won't like, or that are hard work or even may cause a little domestic with other household humans if they are not entirely on board...to which my answer is...get them to read this book of course and then they can understand!

I give you my word that I will not tell you to do anything that I haven't done myself or experienced with a client. 70% of the content of this book is from things I have done wrong at some point and had to deal with, or have done right and it has worked, time and time again. The other 30% is experience gained from and with clients' dogs and helping them to introduce another dog or to improve the dynamics of their existing pack.

Going from one dog to two is hard if you want to get it right. Going from two to three is the biggest jump, it changes everything.

2
Do you really want another dog?

Is it because your first dog is lonely? Or because you think your dog will be happier with another dog to keep it company while you are out?

If the answer is yes to the above, then pass this book on to someone else after you have read the chapter. Yep, I did warn you I was going to be blunt. I'm not here to waste your time.

This is the most common reason why people get another dog and it is the worst reason. There is only one exception to this, and it is only one option to possibly (not a guaranteed way) help your dog's separation anxiety….please note you labelling your dog with separation anxiety does not necessarily mean they have it. Get a professional in to tell you either way before making any big decisions.
Anyway back to the point…why is it the worst reason to get an additional dog? Contrary to popular belief dogs do not need other dogs for company, that's what we are for and what dogs have been selectively bred for years for - to be man's best friend!

If you feel guilty leaving your dog behind when you go to work and if you are away from home regularly for longer than 4 hours, either employ a professional dog walker to help or a neighbour, friend or family member to pop in or dog sit.

If you don't have time for your one dog, how are you going to have time for two? I want you to sit and really think about this. Any new dog, puppy or adult dog will need training, teaching the rules of your house and lifestyle and your existing dog will be a big distraction to both you and the new dog which makes it a lot harder for the new dog to learn what you require. Keep reading to learn more about what I mean.

Think about it, dogs know dog speak, or at least dogs speak the same language, it's easier for them to get along with each other than it is to learn how to read our behaviour and 'language' (commands). You will always be battling against this with any additional dog, whether its dog number 2 or dog number 6 (as it has been recently in my case).

If we put it in human terms – if you were to move on your own right now to China and nobody spoke English, you would have to learn Chinese and would put a lot of effort into doing so, so you could get by comfortably. If, however you moved to China with your friend or family you wouldn't put so much importance on learning the native language as you could always have a conversation with your friend or family. I'm sure eventually you would learn some of the Chinese language and be able to get by, but would still get into conversations with a Chinese person and end up getting a little stuck sometimes because you can always come back to the comfort of your family or friend that lives with you to have a 'normal conversation'. This is a dog or a puppy moving in with its friend/family (your existing dog or dogs), and you are the Chinese people/person.

We need to teach dogs to be bi-lingual but prefer their second language to the first when it counts (i.e., listen to us or read us more than other dogs).

I have so many clients who employed me to help them and train them and their puppy the first time around, and if they got it right, the dog turns out to be a beautiful adult dog, the perfect family member for them and then they go and get another. Despite my warnings about how it will be harder, despite them having done it once already they have some expectation the first dog will 'teach' the second dog how to be good. If anything the opposite is true in most cases. Those niggles that didn't really cause a problem with the first dog (i.e., chasing squirrels in the garden or pulling on lead but its ok because they're only small and can't pull that much), is exactly what the first dog teaches the second, and because it's now two dogs doing it is now a problem, and a hard one to fix. This is because it's something you have to train them not to do individually, and separate from each other first, before then training them together, as they will always feed off each other's energy and have the picture in their mind that they both do this when faced with a squirrel or when they are on lead.

Later in the book, I will give you solutions on how to stop the second picking up on the first's behaviour, but the easiest way is to train them to do something else when faced with the squirrel long before new dog or puppy comes home.

Don't get another dog if you can't:

- If you can't do separate walks with puppy/new dog for a minimum of 10 months or until the dog is mature, and if we are talking about large or giant breeds this maybe 2 years!
- If you can't shut your existing dog in another room, and they are relaxed while you are preoccupied doing something else (not just while you sleep at night).
  You will need this to train puppy and bond with them through play etc. separately.
- If you can't provide as much love and attention to it as you do the other dog or dogs.
- If you can't pay for additional kenneling, house sitting, holiday care when you are away.
- If you can't afford to pay a professional groomer anywhere between every 4-12 weeks depending on coat type if you are looking at a long haired or wirehair breed or a mix of breeds.
- If you can't afford to pay twice as many vet bills, buy twice if not more the number of chews, toys, dog coats, food, etc.
- If you don't have space in your car or vehicle for another dog, this may be an obvious one but many people over-look this matter as a puppy is so tiny when they come home, think about its size as an adult.
- If you can't consider thinking about taking one dog out without the other. The flip side to this is, if your dogs have never been separated, what happens when one of them suddenly dies or needs emergency veterinary care etc. and they are forcibly separated, if they have only ever learned to cope being with each other the one who is left behind will be severely stressed and traumatized. This is a heartbreaking thing to watch which is why I ensure I can say with all my six that they would be happy and content if for whatever reason they ended up being an only dog.

Reading this so far, I'm sure you are thinking why does she have six, or what a hypocrite for telling me not to have another dog. I'm saying it to help you and your existing dog or dogs to help you make the right decision. I have had it all go wrong, I have added a new dog at the wrong time and paid the consequences, not only this I have seen it countless times with clients. Sometimes, unfortunately, it is beyond repair, and we are left with three options when it all goes wrong, none of which is pleasant.

Option 1

Keep both/all dogs, but keep some/all separate for the rest of their lives. This involves numerous and highly managed separate trips out to the garden, many doors being shut or baby gates in the way, making it impossible to take the whole pack on holiday with you or if you leave them all behind putting enough trust into someone who will manage the routine to the letter as you do. This also divides your time even further to ensure all still get cuddles in separate areas of the house and they can never even come nose to nose again. Not to mention separate walks till one or more of them pass over to the rainbow bridge. Most situations that lead to this arise when one or more of the dogs is under the age of 3 years which means many years of this highly stressful arrangement.

Option 2

Rehome one or more dogs
This may mean into rescue or privately or to a friend or family member. Often if they go to a family member, it's harder than you think. Regularly seeing said dog either in person or pictures on social media is the constant reminder of what you feel is your failure to care for that dog.

Option 3

Have the dog euthanized.
Self-explanatory and a horrific and difficult decision to make.

Unfortunately, I have had to do all three of these options in the past, and none were pleasant. In reality, 2 & 3 are the kindest to both you and the remaining dogs, with option 2 being the preference.

I don't mean to be morbid, but these are the facts.

When things are going well, I wouldn't say it's easy! It's hard work, I love each of my dogs and wouldn't want to be without them, but I also know three, four or five dogs for me is a more comfortable number than six, six is manageable, seven is not…but that's just me. We all have different limits. I also know that other factors come into this such as, if any of the following changed about my lifestyle I would not be able to continue with the number I currently have.

If I didn't have a large van for work as well as personal use I wouldn't be able to take my guys on the road with me or on holiday with them all. If my husband Mark and I separated, not only would I not be able to afford the time or money to care for six physically, Mark would have custody of at least two of them, and that would be the best thing for those dogs. If we didn't have the size or layout of the house, we currently have in the location it's in, at least two of our current pack would not cope. I'd like to point out that we don't live in the middle of nowhere, we live in a detached house but only 2 meters away from the next house, and we live in a small village.

Balancing the scales for a multi-dog household is precisely that, a balancing act, for just two dogs not so much but for any more than that it gets a more delicate and finer line between happy and managed and miserable and unmanaged for both the dogs and us.

Despite what you have read already, believe me, I love having multiple dogs! I can't ever imagine just having one, though on the surface there are many benefits to only having one to spend time with and enjoy and train I don't ever think that would be enough for me, I love nothing more than going on long walks with the whole pack and taking them away on holiday to explore new walks and places with them.

This book will give you all the tools you need to ensure you avoid getting to options 1, 2, & 3 if and only if you follow it to the letter.

It's worth remembering that we as people sometimes meet other people whom we instantly dislike, we have no rhyme nor reason and can't explain it but no matter how much someone tells us that the new person is nice, ok, etc. We will never reach the same conclusion, and dogs are often the same. There will always be the minority of dogs that your dog will not get on with, they may appear to like every dog they meet (just as we are all very good at being polite during introductions) but that's a very different thing to suddenly living with one (in which case we would very soon make our feelings known).

Dogs are all born with a specific set of personalities, and although we can mould and shape and influence this they will always have tendencies of the original character they were born with. When you know what to look for you can see glimpses of this from 2-3 weeks of age (more on this later). If you think about humans, some of us are born to be leaders and influence people, and some are not. No matter how many self-help books etc. someone can read, if they have always, from a young age been a bit of a sheep or an unconfident person nothing is going to make them into a real calm and confident leader and vice versa. We can often see this in children too.

Having multiple dogs means different mixes of personalities along with our own and choosing the right mix is key to ensure success and happiness all around.

3
My own furry family

It is not my intention to bore you with the details of all of my dogs, I'm fully aware that we all love to talk about our own dogs. As you progress through the book you will see that I use them as examples regularly to aid in your understanding of the complexities of having multiple dogs. Their personalities, ages, breeds and sexes all make a difference to ensuring things work. All of the information I'm giving about my guys is honest and relevant to help you with your dogs. You will also notice that I mention Mark a few times throughout the publication, Mark is my wonderful and supporting Husband.

Introductions to my guys

A break away with the dogs for a week in October 2017 confirmed my decision to have Ripple. The litter was born when we were away on this break, and of course, I knew that I was interested in a bitch should there be one within the litter, but was unsure if having six dogs again was right for the gang and me at that point in all of our lives. We went to the same place with the dogs we had been to previously. The difference in just 8 months of three of the dogs' stamina and energy levels on longer walks than their usual walks was astounding, I would go as far as saying it was reduced by almost 50%. It's so sad. I hate that they are aging but count my lucky stars that I share my life with such amazing beings. I realised I would need an up and coming dog to help with training client's dogs and to lighten the load on the others. I made notes on all of my dogs (and our other animals) at this point including ages (of course they are now older), including pros and cons of introducing Ripple and here are my notes below.

Mica (AKA Mica moo cow) 10 & 3/4year old Springer girl.

Mica was Mark's dog when we met, and despite being a Springer she is a very calm dog, reasonably aloof with new people (unless they have a ball to offer), but she loves to play fetch!
She's an itchy dog with a quite a few environmental allergies, but she copes with this well.

Over the previous couple of months, we had come to realise she was rapidly going deaf, I'd guess at the moment she is about 80% deaf, but the whistle is still reaching her ears on walks which is excellent (as long as it's not in high wind). In her body and mind, she is very active and fit, as much as when she was much younger.
She would play fetch all day if we let her, and for this reason, balls are not allowed in the house as she never gives up trying to get us to play if one is on offer.

Mica primarily works with me with reactive dogs as a distraction dog (both on and off lead as she will not approach them). I usually use Mica once the dog in training has progressed quite far in their programme and use her to chase after her ball at a distance from the dog and work closer. Spaniel movement is swift and exciting for many dogs, so she provides an excellent training opportunity for clients to work with their dog to relax when this is happening, just like they would see on an everyday walk. Mica is also instrumental with adolescent playful and excitable dogs as she will ignore them and not encourage their playful and sometimes rude behaviour. This gives me and the client opportunity to practice recall away from Mica (which we can then start to apply to other dogs). With Mica's hearing deteriorating, her off lead walks without a toy are going to be limited more and more once she cannot hear the whistle. However, if there is a toy or ball she never takes her eyes off me in the expectation of play, so while her body and mind are still able to, she will continue to help some dogs. Toys can create conflict with some other dogs, so she will soon, sadly not be able to work with me in these cases.

With Ripple, I'm not expecting any conflict or issues where Mica is concerned. Mica will ignore Ripple for the most part, which isn't a bad thing. When Ripple progresses to go on walks with Mica, I will concentrate on Ripple being focused on me while Mica does her usual spaniel circles off the lead and chasing after the ball/toy. This is very exciting for young dogs to try and chase, which can cause frustration issues such as barking and yapping because Ripple will not be able to keep up (though she may be able to when she is fully grown). She's a very rare spaniel, calm and collected for the most part. Mica is a star!

Fern (AKA the worm). 4.5 years of age and at this point our youngest pooch.

She's a Miniature Longhaired Dachshund bitch, my most challenging but also the most loving and playful dog.

She is a 'reactive dog' yes, shock horror I am a trainer, and I haven't managed to 'fix' my own dogs behaviour! That's because there is no such thing as 'fixing' emotional behaviours, and certainly not with Fern. She is reactive to maybe 1 in 15 people out and about if they try to interact with her...she will walk past or sit in front of them if they are preoccupied and would appear to be a 'normal dog' (whatever that is). Her main issue is indoors, primarily in the house, people coming through doorways, including familiar people (not just the front door). When I say reactive, for her this means barking, charging up and lunging at the said person, she has never gone to bite or put her teeth on a person. She will soon calm down and often actively seek attention from these people within a couple of minutes of barking.

Why is she like this? Her mum was a singleton puppy. Because she never had littermates to compete with she never learned how to deal with frustration, and displayed behaviours such as, for example barking at me when I came downstairs from the toilet or whenever I left the room and re-entered the living room where she was. I stayed for a week at the breeder's house as a guest.... Fern's mum would not only bark at me every time I came back in sight, but she would carry on to bark for what was an excessive amount of time (often 15-20 minutes) despite the breeder doing her best to try to stop her. The first behaviour that Fern and her littermates learned was from their mother (this is sometimes called imprinting) and these behaviours are so ingrained that they are almost as strong as instinct. When Fern joined our family, I have to admit I was at a stage in my CPD training where I was overconfident. Though my peers all said (and the science said) that you cannot 're-train what is imprinted' I was determined to prove them wrong…with enough work I was convinced that I could do it, not only that but once Fern was 'better' I had planned to breed from her! (I'm cringing at myself writing this! She has since been spayed). This is why I'm often harping on about how the mothers behaviour is everything. Hopefully, you understand a little more why now.

In particular training environments, she will have the odd bark at another dog if they are too close or barking at her, but this is getting less and less and usually when I'm distracted and in an area with a lot of dogs in close proximity, such as a training class or competition.

The fact is, I weighed up my options. Fern is the youngest, so I couldn't wait until Fern is no longer with us to get a new furry team member. Will Fern's behaviour have in impact on Ripple? Yes, it will, but I am determined to minimise this as much as possible. I made mistakes with Fern that I have learned from which has made me a better, more sympathetic (and more humble) trainer. I take comfort in knowing Fern is only 10% reactive compared to what she used to be and that she is better behaved than she would be in 90% of households.

Fern is managed well around her primary triggers and of course puppies, or impressionable young dogs are more likely to learn all the 'bad behaviours' rather than the good. Often more adrenaline and fun is involved in the bad…so my biggest challenge when introducing Ripple was that she wouldn't bond too closely to Fern (the more bonded they are, the more likely she is to follow in her footsteps) and that she doesn't get exposed to Fern's behaviour without management as much as possible. Not an easy feat!

It has been a long journey with Fern, and we have both grown in our journey, there have been many tears, of joy and frustration and upset. She started showing the behaviours at around 14-16 weeks of age, just about when the hormones start to kick in, and I put a lot of my pressure on myself as I felt everyone was judging me… 'ha! She can't be a very good trainer if she's made her puppy reactive'. 'Some trainer she is' etc. Which would then make me more determined to prove everyone wrong (interspersed with many moments of wanting to go and hide under a rock). I learned to breathe, ignore the judgments and take every day as it comes, good and bad and rejoice in all the little victories. Many have met Fern and when I have explained about her have asked me if I'm talking about the same dog?

Fern does come out and help me with select reactive dogs and puppies who are scared of other dogs, meets clients and is happy to have a fuss from them.

I compete with Fern in dog sports, she is the first female Dachshund to achieve her Level 6 (the highest level) KC Rally Title, she has her KC canine good citizen award to Gold level. Last year she successfully competed as part of our Dachshund Obreedience Team which we made it to Crufts 2018 for the final - and we were placed fourth! She enjoys her training and competing, and this has helped her confidence around people.

Fern is a very happy dog overall, very playful and she is 'Daddy's princess' (very spoilt by my husband, Mark). She can be pushy at times with new dogs entering the house so I know she will want to 'tell Ripple off' before Ripple had the chance to settle, so I plan to introduced Fern to Ripple while Fern is on a light lead and with lots of cheese to hand (Fern's favourite). I am confident Fern wouldn't attack Ripple (or any dog for that matter) as she is what I call 'all mouth no trousers'. If left to her own devices she would charge up to her, give a quick grumble then back off and all would be well in Fern's mind. I never want to encourage this behaviour, nor do I want her to scare such a young puppy.

I was a little reluctant to be so open about this but feel honesty is the best policy. Hopefully, this will help you understand some of the content of this book, and help you re-evaluate if you are considering getting another dog if your existing dog has any annoying or undesirable habits. Without prudent management, you will end up with twice (if not three times) the issue.
The Worm is undoubtedly a character, but well-loved and happy!

Merlin (AKA the Goon!) - age 9.5 years, Flatcoat Retriever

He had spinal surgery at 3.5 years. His spine has been fusing together since this age, and he has been suffering from a disc infection for almost 3 years now. Touch wood for now at least it doesn't appear to be bothering him. It's incredible that he is still with us, and still a very happy bouncy boy with a real zest for life (which is why he is called the goon). The goon managed to achieve his Level 2 title in KC Rally before retiring due to his health (and the higher levels involving jumps). He has helped rehabilitate countless dog-reactive dogs, helped many puppies realise that big black furry beasts are nothing to be scared of and also helped shy/uncertain dogs recognise that town centre environments are not as scary as they thought. He continues to do this with vigour when he is in good form with his health. He is a 'Flatcoat Retriever' a breed that sadly rarely makes 10 years of age due to the high rate of cancer in the breed. Saying this, Merlin is by no means ready to slow down and enjoys his role of 'Uncle Mer' with puppies particularly. He is a dog that would never say boo to a goose, extremely sociable and loves nothing more than a good fuss. The drawback I would say with a tiny puppy is Merlin's size, he's 2 inches taller than the breed standard, and he can be a little clumsy with it. I often joke that because he was reared alongside Miniature Dachshunds both with his breeder and with me, that he thinks he's a Dachshund as Merlin has never quite realised his size (especially when he likes to walk through my legs, at just 5ft I have to stand on my tip toes!). He has always been as gentle as possible with little puppies, but I plan to err on the side of caution and keep interactions supervised with Ripple in the early days, keeping excitement/arousal levels low when Ripple and Merlin are loose together. Merlin is a great role model for a new puppy as he is confident in all situations, nothing phases him, he loves everyone and everything. I accept sadly that Merlin's health could go downhill at any time and would like him to pass on his beautiful nature and confidence to Ripple. Hopefully, he will be with us for a good while yet.

Ziggy (AKA - Zigalig and Ratbag), Age 12 and he is a Miniature Longhaired Dachshund

Ziggy suffers from a collapsible trachea, epilepsy, a grade 2 heart murmur, arthritic hips and is currently going blind due to a genetic disorder called PRA, this is very late onset, so in many ways, we have been lucky that he didn't go blind many years ago. Ziggy is the happiest little dog you will ever meet, bouncy and friendly with lots of energy despite his age and health concerns. His sight is expected to have gone entirely by the end of 2018, currently he has no peripheral vision and is blind in low light. He has successfully competed in KC Rally and was one competition short of gaining his level 6 title before I retired him due to his vision and age. He also was part of our Obreedience Team previously, and he retired at the finals at Crufts 2017 with a fab third place. A very sociable little chap with dogs and people, if not a little needy. Over the years he has helped with countless puppies' socialisation and with reactive dogs as a stooge dog.

He really does need to take a back seat and retire properly from 'work' though, again due to his age and deteriorating sight. I'm not sure he would agree! Ratbag is the most unphotogenic dog in history, and such a needy sod, but we love him. I expect Ziggy to perform his usual duties of 'Uncle Zig' with Ripple (after all he has done this now many times as he is the eldest). He will be a good role model for her, he is still a playful character, so I will restrict this to some extent with Ripple so she bonds with humans a little more. Having the distraction of so many other dogs will be a big draw to her to bond with them (as they speak the same language, it comes so much easier) rather than us, so a lot of time at least in the initial weeks and months will be spent with Ripple with us and separate from the other dogs. At no point will Ripple be left unattended and loose with the other guys to restrict the amount they bond together and have influence over her while she's still maturing.

Moss (AKA Mossymoo & Moss the boss) Age 6, Miniature Longhaired Dachshund

Moss is Ripple's dad. I bred him myself but sadly lost his mother the beautiful Jazz in the process. Countless sleepless nights hand rearing him and his four brothers was hard work but so worth it. He is a very calm, loving and confident dog (except when on off lead walks, where he is a busy lad). Moss helps out with puppy training, socialisation, adolescents and reactive dogs. He was the first Dachshund of all six varieties to gain his KC Rally Level 6 title, and he is also part of our Obreedience Team for the second year running. He has recently become a paid model for a very well-known dog food brand. He's a fast learner and loves learning new tricks with the clicker. I won't bore you with many of his other achievements but it's safe to say, in 6 years, we have done a lot together. When Ripple arrives, I expect Moss will have a little sniff and then take a back seat for a while as he likes to figure people and dogs out, in time he will become playful with Ripple but also gently ascertain some boundaries. I will limit the amount of play. I plan to use Moss as an excellent role model in social environments as he is the type of dog you can take anywhere and he will relax and almost not notice he is there. Saying this, I will be taking Ripple to plenty of places without any of the other dogs so she can grow in confidence on her own and not rely on the others. Moss has recently been joining me on carriage drives with my pony Billy, and I plan for Ripple to also do this, so initially at least both Ripple and Moss will come together so he can show her the ropes. Understandably Moss is very close to my heart, as are they all, but a very special bond was formed throughout the hand-rearing process. I had always wanted a little girl out of Jazz as she had such an excellent temperament that could be passed on to the next generation but alas she only gave me boys. Finally, with Ripple's arrival, I get my wish (or as close as possible to it).

Dobi - 14 year old British short-haired cat

Dobi is a little slow but he always has been, bless him, he's not bothered by dogs. He is neither the swipe at them or a run from them type of cat...more of a disapproving look and slowly walks away kind. He has plenty of places to get away from the dogs if he chooses. I expect Ripple will be curious and try to play but then soon learn that he's not much fun just like our others have. Ziggy and Merlin had never lived with a cat when I moved in with Mark (and Dobi and Mica), but they settled in a relatively short period. The importance being that Dobi had the choice to get away from them if and when he felt he needed or wanted to.

Billy - 13 year old Fell Pony gelding

Billy is used to dogs and likes a little sniff of them initially which can be a little confronting to little dogs, he may be a pony, but he does have a big black head which could be a bit scary to one so small. Once he has said hello with a sniff, he ignores them.   Ripple will be in my arms to start with when meeting Billy, from a distance and gradually closer if she is relaxed, slowly working to be on the floor (on a lead, and when Billy is tied up). As I said before - I would like Ripple to join me on carriage drives with Billy, taking in the sights and smells on the country lanes and tracks. So a gradual introduction to him with plenty of reassurance and rewards will help her to relax around Billy and become confident around 'big black scary things'. This will also help her generalise this rule to other creatures that she may encounter through her life. It's important to remember that dogs struggle to 'read' black animals, whether it be black dogs, cows, cats, etc. as their face is in shadow and this can then cause insecurities around such animals.

4

The law and your responsibilities if living in the UK

Some may surprise you so please do not skip what you may think is a boring chapter.

The five freedoms

Animal Welfare Act 2006 introduced an essential concept for pet owners and those responsible for domestic animals, e.g., breeders, those who have working animals or farm animals in England and Wales.

Preventing animals suffering: If this advice is not followed or the animal's needs are not being met, then action can be taken whether through a formal warning or in some cases a prosecution.

What does the law actually say?
Section 9 of the Animal Welfare Act places a duty of care on people to ensure they take reasonable steps in all the circumstances to meet the welfare needs of their animals to the extent required by good practice.

What does this mean for those responsible for animals?
In short it means they must take positive steps to ensure they care for their animals properly and in particular must provide for the five welfare needs, which are:

1. Need for a suitable environment.
2. Need for a suitable diet.
3. Need to be able to exhibit normal behaviour patterns.
4. Need to be housed with, or apart, from other animals.
5. Need to be protected from pain, suffering, injury, and disease.

I would like to bring your attention to number four. I'm assuming by buying this book that you are a responsible dog owner and meeting your dog's needs. Number four is particularly relevant when we are considering adding to our doggy family. The need to be housed with or APART from other animals…if two dogs do not get on then not only do you need to consider your own needs and the dogs involved but also the implications with the law. The same applies if you have other pets/animals who are stressed in the presence of your dog or dogs.

The need to be housed WITH other dogs isn't so relevant, as dogs do not have a NEED for their own kind if they have us (unless you have a dog who did not have any positive contact with humans before 12 weeks of age). Again the meaning of the need to be housed WITH other animals is more relevant to birds, goats, horses, guinea pigs, etc. as they are less domesticated and thrive off the company of their own species.

The Law

The Law and Dogs in the UK is continually changing, and not in favour of us multidog owners. Many councils now have enforced local bylaws that in public parks only four dogs per person are allowed (regardless of size, obedience or if on or off lead), this is worth considering if you are getting number 5 or above. Or if you plan to travel within the UK with your dogs on holiday as your holiday destination may have this rule in place. The fact is the more dogs you have, the more likely they are to cause a nuisance, or noise disturbance when someone rings the doorbell, two dogs barking are louder than one, and yes, I admit it I cringe when our doorbell goes as it sounds like I have 20 dogs, not 6!

The law applies to all breeds of dogs

It's against the law to let a dog be dangerously out of control anywhere, such as:
In a public place.
In a private place, e.g., a neighbour's house or garden.

In the owner's home.

Some types of dogs are banned.

Your dog is considered dangerously out of control if it:
Injures someone.
Makes someone worried that it might injure them.

A court could also decide that your dog is dangerously out of control if any of the following apply:
It attacks someone's animal.
The owner of an animal thinks they could be injured if they tried to stop your dog from attacking their animal.
A farmer is allowed to kill your dog if it's worrying livestock.

Penalties

You can get an unlimited fine or be sent to prison for up to 6 months (or both) if your dog is dangerously out of control. You may not be allowed to own a dog in the future, and your dog may be destroyed.

If you let your dog injure someone you can be sent to prison for up to 5 years or fined (or both). If you deliberately use your dog to injure, someone, you could be charged with 'malicious wounding'.
If you allow your dog to kill someone you can be sent to prison for up to 14 years or get an unlimited fine (or both).
If you allow your dog to injure an assistance dog (e.g., a guide dog), you can be sent to prison for up to 3 years or fined (or both).

The laws that apply to the above, of which you can be prosecuted under are - The Dangerous dogs act and the Control of dogs act. These laws apply to ALL dogs, not just the banned breeds

You must have a dog breeding licence if either:
You run a business that breeds and sells dogs.
You breed 5 or more litters in a year and sell any of the puppies.

Contact your local council to check if you need a licence or for information about costs.

Noise complaints

While dogs are allowed to bark, they are not allowed to bark so that it causes a nuisance. It is a matter of fact, and the degree in each case and factors that may be taken into account include the volume, duration of the barking and the time of day it happens. The test is whether it is of a nature which makes it intrusive or irritating.
If a complaint is made to a local Council, they have a duty to investigate. The Council may serve a Noise Abatement Notice, and if the barking continues then, they may prosecute under the Environmental Protection Act 1990. The likely penalty is a fine.
The neighbour may also take action themselves.

Please note that the above summary only relates to the law in England and Wales. You must not rely on it as constituting legal advice, and so for specific guidance on your particular dog law issue I would recommend visiting doglaw.co.uk or contacting Trevor Cooper at Trevor Cooper and co dog law solicitors.

Identification (ID)

In the UK, the Control of Dogs Order 1992 states that any dog in a public place must wear a collar with the name and address (including postcode) of the owner engraved or written on it, or engraved on a tag. Failure to do so can incur a fine of up to £5000! Please note that the ID should be on the collar, so if your dog is only walked on a harness, a collar and tag/ID should still be worn.
A public place also covers when your dog is in your vehicle.
Exceptions to identification laws apply to working dogs when they are actually working and for assistance dogs.
It's also worth noting that if you let others walk or take your dogs off your property without correct ID and they are caught they will be the person or persons liable to pay the fine.
Contrary to popular belief, the ID rules are not in place for us to get our dogs back if they are lost. Yes, it serves this purpose too, but the rules are in place for liability. If your dog causes an accident, you or the person in charge of the dog at the time is liable for any damage. Most pet insurance policies cover you for public liability, as do some home insurance policies. If in doubt check! Failing that, the Dogs Trust offer a yearly membership for £25-30 which will cover you for instances such at this.

Microchipping

All owners must ensure their dog is microchipped and their details are kept up to date. Not only will this mean the UK's 8.5 million dogs can be returned to their owners more quickly if they wander too far from home, but it will also make it easier to track down the owners of dogs that carry out attacks on people.
Breeders must now have puppies microchipped by the age of 8 weeks (before leaving for new homes).

5
Existing dog issues

The following issues with existing dogs are the most common that if not dealt with before a new puppy is introduced will become a problem when the new dog joins in.
I cannot stress this point enough as it's the most common category I am faced with professionally with multidog households.

Any of the following may only be mildly annoying with one dog but guaranteed to become a real nuisance when adding more dogs to the mix.

Barking excessively or for a prolonged period at the doorbell

Pulling on lead

Not coming back when called off the lead

Barking in the garden

Barking at people passing the house

Any inappropriate barking other than listed above.

Barking, lunging, aggression or frustration toward or other dogs when on lead or off. The same goes for the opposite issue – your dog being fearful and trying to run away from other dogs when on lead or off, same applies to people or livestock

Chasing lunging or fear of traffic, people, cyclists, joggers, children

Jumping up on people, either out on walks or visitors to the house

It's worth mentioning that all dogs need to express normal behaviour and this includes barking, usual barking would be barking to alert you of someone at the door or to alert you to an intruder or visitor, barking in excitement (within reason) and vocalizing during play. The more dogs you have, the more barking and noise you can expect, this is fact, but we do need to be mindful of visitors, neighbours and the dogs' excitement levels.

Exercise/homework for you for the next week

A dog diary

Make a note of how much time you spend each day doing the following

- Cuddling or chilling with your dog, this could be in front of the TV, when you're on your phone on social media or watching YouTube, on the laptop and your dog is present, if your dog is lucky enough to come to work with you or you work from home and your dog is in the same room.
- How long you walk your dog for and at what times, what they do on the walk that you like to enjoy, what they do that you don't want so much and how often this happens. E.g., if your dog pulls, is it constant, how much of the walk they are on lead, is it just on the way out, only on the way back, just when you see another dog/person/horse, etc.
- How many times do you need to call your dog back before it comes?
- How many times do you play with your dog, for how long and how do you play?
- If its muddy how long does it take for you to towel them or wash them off?
- If your dog needs grooming brushing, how long do you spend doing this?
- List your dog's five favourite things to do, and this may include having a treat, a walk, playing, chilling with you, swimming, etc.

Has your lifestyle changed in any way since you had your previous dog, mainly if you had him from a puppy, what did you do with him when he was a puppy? If you are happy with their level of sociability is it something you can replicate?

List the five things that bug you about your dog, including the little things, the ones that cause you to roll your eyes at or you have the passing thought that I would be a bit easier if they didn't do. On the flip side is there anything your dog could or does do that would make your life easier? This could include getting you a beer from the fridge, or fetching the remote control.

Average working day for me and my guys (without a puppy)

Wake up at 6 am. Dogs let out into the garden to the toilet. I fuss each of them after I let them back in (around 10 minutes in the garden). I have a cup of tea (or two) and get on with some admin work on the PC with the dogs relaxing at my feet until around 8.30 am. I load two or three dogs into the van, and we go about our day training clients and their dogs until around 12 pm all dogs who are with me will have some individual time out of the van with me, being used as distraction dogs. The entire time they are out of the vehicle for each session is around 10 minutes. Lunchtime walks for 30-45 minutes, depending on who I have and where we are and what type of exercise is appropriate.
Occasionally I may have client's dogs to walk at lunchtime in which case my guys who are on the road with me at the time will get an hour's walk with clients' dogs. I will pop home, swap dogs over and progress on to more training sessions with clients which will also finish with a walk. I'm usually home around 4/5 pm and will either sit on the PC doing admin or daylight dependent, I may spend some time with my pony (50/50 if I take some dachshunds with me, if we are driving in the carriage then at least one (sometimes three) dachshunds will come along on the carriage for the ride). The hours that I am not home, my husband will be at home with the others, he spoils them, and they get lots of play and attention. This differs from day to day. Sometimes I will be training or be playing with my guys in the evenings sometimes we just relax on the sofa together. My dogs are fed once per day, usually in the evening. They typically go out for last toilets in the garden around 10-11pm.
In the summer I spend around an hour a week grooming all five, in the winter when its muddy, 20-30 minutes per day as they are all long haired. Plus time is taken to wash dog coats and towels; more bedding changes from the van cages in winter too.

Tweaks I could/should make - improve Moss's recall off a scent (hunting), Fern's barking at visitors, Ziggy yapping if he's been shut outside for more than 5 minutes. Merlin's pushiness for attention when we have visitors and Mica's tendency to bark/chase in the garden at dusk/dark. All issues are pretty minor compared to what they were in the past, we have improved them, but I should do more to prevent puppy Ripple picking up on these behaviours.

They are all very similar in their likes and dislikes, they all enjoy playing with toys, but some more than others. All enjoy training. Some enjoy playing fetch, and some prefer tug of war. They all love their food and all love to sniff out hidden treats. All love individual attention, all love a good fuss on the sofa, and of course, all love a walk, particularly new places to explore. It's only Ziggy that doesn't enjoy swimming, the others love it. I would guess that without the five dogs I would likely have at least two more hours in the day and a new puppy will double this for a while so it's as much about considering financial cost as it is time, have I got the time to spare? More time costs to consider, 'retraining' some unwanted behaviours before Ripple's arrival.

Solutions and management pre-puppy arrival

'Birds of a feather flock together'

If your dog has any of the issues I have described, I would urge you to get help from a qualified professional trainer or behaviourist to at the very least improve it before pup comes home. Honestly, the money, time and effort you put in now will be well worth the investment and save you a dog's lifetime of stress and frustration. If the issue you are facing is a real bugbear, whatever you have been doing to 'fix' the problem apparently hasn't worked so far, or it would not be an issue now would it…harsh I know but true.

Which brings me to a point I should have mentioned before – if you are getting a puppy because you want to 'get it right this time round' because you didn't last time…it is almost impossible when you are still experiencing the issue with the previous dog, and without a mixture of help and strict management, it will get worse and new pupster will become a pro at performing the issue often as well as if not better than the previous dog!

I have been guilty of this, hands up really, I have. Especially in my early days of learning how to be a dog trainer, sitting in many courses and seminars swearing to do it this new way the next time and getting puppy broody with it. Honestly, I know I'm going on and on about this, but please at least work at improving your current dog or pack of dogs before new puppy arrives.

Proper dog training means setting a dog up for success, and not setting them up to fail.

You will be setting yourself up to fail if you don't tackle whatever issues you are currently faced with.

'You are the company, you keep. A chain is only as strong as its weakest link'

Yep, some old cheesy quotes, but this is your pack we are talking about.

Guaranteed if just one dog likes to bark more than the others, the new one will join in, because that's what dogs do! They will not look at the calmest dog and follow that one and copy its behaviour. Having calmer or nice role model adult dogs will give you the best chance to train puppy to do the same.

Management

'Better to be alone than in the wrong company'

Management is about manipulating the environment/situation and protecting the puppy from being exposed to unwanted behaviours performed by the other dogs, or protecting the dog who is being managed from performing unwanted behaviours. Management is not training, but it is an extremely useful tool. In some cases a management solution to a dog not coming back off lead would be to keep the dog on lead or if a dog is reactive or barking at other dogs the management solution would be to avoid other dogs.

While none of these solutions are 'curing' the dog of the issue, it is preventing the dog from practicing the wrong behaviour. This provides a window of opportunity to work on replacing the unwanted behaviour with a new and desirable behaviour as and when you can control the environment and set the dog up for success. Without management as part of any behaviour modification plan you will fail.

Just like us if we want to break a bad habit it isn't productive to go back to the old habit between practicing the new habit. For example let's look at smoking, when a person quits smoking they try to replace the time that they would smoke with something else, this may be having a mint, or distracting themselves in some other way while the cravings are at the forefront of their mind. If they sometimes had a cigarette and sometimes didn't, you wouldn't consider them to be an 'ex-smoker' would you? A dog who has practiced a behaviour just a handful of times is a lot easier to train to do an alternative behaviour, than a dog who has had years and years of practising the wrong thing on what could be a daily basis. Patience is key, remember that training takes time and management solutions will help you in your journey to success.

I have one dog in my pack who barks at new people when they enter through doorways. Her mother did the same, she is (still) much worse than my dog, Fern. Fern has learnt this behaviour from just weeks old she is programmed to do the same, many hours work, training, behaviour modification, ongoing behavior medication has reduced this greatly, but I admit defeat, I will never 'fix' this issue. She is now 5 years of age, so she is very well practised. Because this is an issue that is primarily displayed in the house, it's one of the biggest factors of consideration when I decided to have another dog. Management is going to be 80% if not more of what I will be doing with Ripple and Fern when visitors arrive. I will either have Ripple out of the house (maybe in the garden or in my van for a short period) to allow Fern to say hello in her initially loud way, and then settle with the visitor before allowing Ripple into the house. This way I am shielding Ripple from learning to bark at new people coming through doorways, giving her the opportunity to learn new people are ok. If I failed to put management solutions in place, particularly for this scenario I would guarantee that Ripple would bark at people coming through doorways, and likely before the age of 6 months.

6
Multi-dog exercises/games - make your life easier

First things first - not only does each dog need to know its individual name, but you need to decide on a collective name. For example, I use 'doggo's', so doggos come, doggos wait, etc. This is when you want all of the dogs to do the same thing. Let's face it, I wouldn't have my guys return to me quickly when off lead on a walk is I was calling six names with come or here between each one! I use a verbal group/collective name or a whistle. I have specific whistles/pitches for individual dogs, namely the two gundogs but I use a different pitch of whistle for the collective recall.

General manners

As I've mentioned before, dogs only do what pays. So if you give attention to the pushiest dog, the dog who barges their way to the front this behaviour pays and will encourage the others to do the same which in time becomes a nightmare. Make an effort to interact/pay the calmer dogs, for being patient, for sitting back, for being good. This practice, if done by everyone in the household will make everything else so much easier. Patience pays, pushing does not.

Life sucks sometimes

Although it's tempting to give all dogs a treat if you give one dog a treat...this isn't great practice. Your dogs need to learn that sometimes they miss out and that's ok! If we always treat them all the same, this can encourage pushy, possessive behaviour on the one occasion they have something that the others don't. Life isn't fair sometimes, and that's just the way things are.

Body blocking

To help with general management and teaching these games a useful tool to have is the use of your body. Dogs will use their body and posture to block the route of others. This is particularly useful around doorways etc. Try to refrain from using your hands. Dogs will understand better when you use your body rather than your hands. After all dogs do not use their paws in this way to communicate with each other.
Doing these exercises will not only help the pup and its frustration levels but also make your life easier and help gel the pack together in the right way.

Group off/leave it

'Back Up', don't go any further or get off that item of furniture. Particularly useful for when they are about to all go and chase after a rabbit, or they are all huddled in your spot on the sofa. Start with this command individually. I usually start with teaching them to leave a digestive biscuit or similar low-value item on the floor, then rewarding them with something better (never giving them the biscuit or item I am teaching them to leave) and work up to higher value items from there.

Wait or stay with individual recall/release

This is when all dogs wait, but you only call one dog to you while the others wait in position. This needs to be built up, so start with two dogs, one being your most steady dog (the one who is the most reliable with the wait command and another, starting with calling the less reliable dog while the more steady dog stays in position, don't forget to return and reward the dog for not coming when you called the other, this is more important than rewarding the dog who you called. Build this up gradually, make it easy, stay in the house or garden with short distances.

Applications - doorways, putting on harnesses or coats, checking dogs for injuries, training sessions without barriers (so you can train or play with one dog while the others wait patiently without being restrained or separated).

Treat labels

A similar and beneficial thing to practice from the start with any number of dogs is to label them when giving a treat...say their individual name before giving a treat and ignoring other dogs trying to get in on the action, enough repetition of this stops them jumping all over each other for treats. This stops the piranha like jaws nipping at your fingers when you are giving treats.

If you are giving attention on one dog, a fuss or stroke and others try and get in on the action, ignore the other dog, maybe even make more of a fuss of the dog you were initially giving attention to. Once the second dog has got the idea that there's no attention on offer for them and walked off to settle or do something else, this is when you stop giving attention to the first dog and call the second over (in other words you are rewarding the second dog for walking away and not pestering you).

Musical Bowls

All dogs sit (or down or a position of your choosing) and wait for food to be placed down, you stand all the way up and give a command to release in your own time (this should be standard practice anyway). As each dog finishes, they wait by their own bowl until everyone has finished, you then give a release command to allow them to lick each other's dishes. This practice is particularly useful for those dogs who gobble their food in the hope of moving on to the next dogs' food. I find in most cases this slows down their eating time because that way they don't have to wait as long between finishing their own food and licking the other dogs' bowls. Gobbling it fast doesn't pay.

Dessert

In place of musical bowls. All dogs sit (or alternative action) wait, and you release them to eat, the difference here is you then teach the dogs to go somewhere else (away from the food bowls) once they have finished. This may be to the door or their beds etc. and you give them a small morsel of a higher value treat such as a little bit of liver or chicken. If they don't go to where they are meant to and instead decide to harass the other dogs and their bowls they don't get any dessert.

7

What your puppy must learn and be taught individually

Loose lead walking, wait, how to deal with frustration, recall, autofocus, other dogs are ok but not as fun as you, how to be alone – away from the other dogs. Individual socialisation, travelling, vets trips/pub trips, etc.

In other words EVERYTHING!

To force this point home a little more, Ripple will not be out on walks with the rest of the gang (as in the whole pack) until she is over a year old. I will take her on walks with the others individually or a couple of them with her, but in the right situations where I know the others don't have any issues or bad habits. It's almost like convincing her that the others are all 'perfect' (ha-ha far from it, I may be a trainer, but I am human and not perfect either). I do this by only showing their best behaviours. This in its self will not train her how to be good, rather give me the opportunity to train her and reward her for the best behaviours so she isn't tempted to 'join in' with whatever the others are doing wrong as it looks like more fun.

Think about how much time you spent with your first dog when they arrived, how many places you took them, how much time you spent training them, playing with them, just you and your dog against the world. This is what you need to aim for with your new pup, everything solo, to get that all-important bond with you. While not forgetting you still have at least one older dog who requires you to meet its needs as you do now (or maybe a little more than now).

Yes, there are things you will be able to involve your existing dog or dogs with the new pup, but first, the puppy has to learn to do these alone (with you but without the others).

Always ask yourself 'how is Fido in this situation normally' Fido being your older/existing dog and if the answer isn't exactly what you want then that's not the dog to take with you while you are taking the pup to learn what you do want in that environment.

A couple of examples for my pack would be Moss is the best at settling in social environments such as cafés and pubs so Ripple could join him for things like that. Mica, however, stresses in these environments, so I wouldn't take Ripple and Mica together in this kind of situation until either Ripple is confident and mature (i.e. over 12 months) or I have worked with Mica, and she is more settled in this environment. Training and management is everything.

Another thing to consider here is your stress level, patience and time to do this. Guaranteed if you go ahead and get another puppy, there will be points where you will question why you ever did it, this is normal! I can remember getting to this point a good few times when Ripple was between the ages of 12 and 20 weeks. For larger breeds many owners will still be questioning themselves when pup is over 18 months (larger breeds take a lot longer to mature and are bigger and heavier so can cause more havoc than small breeds). This is not to say when I was wondering why I got a sixth dog that I didn't love Ripple, nor did I regret having her at any point, it was just a stage we went through. Sometimes it can be outside influences such as work or family issues that add to the stress and being concerned that you are not doing enough for pup, in other times it can be that pup is going through a developmental stage that is proving testing to the owner....normal!

8
Functional characters

This chapter will cause some unease, particularly amongst any modern trainers reading this. It is controversial. My original outline for this book did not include this chapter to avoid the havoc it may cause when published. But my brave pants are on!
The more I wrote, the more I realized I couldn't put this book out there and miss out such key information, so on my head be it.

Before I go any further, I would like to give you a little background information. I have been on both sides of the fence, the 'dominance in dogs theory' fence. We trainers regularly will have heated discussions on this subject.

Many years ago, before my professional training days, I was led by others to believe that we must always be 'pack leader', be almost harsh with our dogs and 'show them who is boss' including with force when needed, I hold my hands up, I was one of those people! After taking the decision to have one of my wonderful dogs put to sleep for aggression issues (and all those 'dominance theory' methods hadn't worked) I started to question them and read a book called 'Dominance Fact or Fiction' by Barry Eaton which influenced me right over to the other side. No such thing as dominance! Fast forward a year or two and I met a good friend and fellow trainer who had what I believed were some 'out there' beliefs about hierarchy within dogs, and she took me to watch some captive wolves feeding on a pony carcass. Mainly so she could prove a point. I watched how they took turns on this carcass, how some lingered over certain parts of the animal, some guarded their 'share' others tried to muscle in and then backed off when reprimanded. I then spent a few hours observing them, and their interactions with each other and I couldn't argue….but yes these were wolves, not dogs. We do not have wild wolves living in our homes with us. The reason I couldn't argue with her was that I knew a family of Rottweiler mixes, all who lived outside, loose with each other and who were regularly fed from one food source… in this case a black bin liner full of school meal leftovers, I knew each of their personalities very well and how they chose to feed. When watching the wolves I may as well have been watching Macy, Rocko, Rizla, and Tizer (the Rotty mixes - Macy and Rocko brother and sister, Rizla father, Tizer - Macys son and brother to my beloved Bella who I had euthanized).

Science tells us that dogs and wolves are genetically 98% identical, the two species can mate with each other and produce fertile offspring. Dogs have been selectively bred for thousands of generations over thousands of years to be compatible with humans and live alongside us harmoniously, this means dogs and wolves are not the same, but they are also from essentially the same genetic makeup.

How much does this play a part in our daily lives with our dogs?….If you just have one dog I'm not sure this chapter is particularly relevant if you are going to stick to one canine and you don't have any dreams or aspirations for it other than for it to be a great family dog.

Yes, the following information can well help you pick a suitable first dog for you, or help you assess or categorize your current dog, but it will unlikely make too much difference to you. Singular dogs adapt to most of the functional characters depending on what we are doing or how we react to certain situations, they don't particularly have to perform any of the characters well, as they are only responsible for themselves and those of you with just one dog will be able to manage one dog with relative ease.

So there is a natural hierarchy between dogs, it's not always as linear as we think, and age, experience, and trauma will affect this.
Do I think we, as humans need to worry about being a pack leader? No. We rule the world. We control when they go out to exercise, to the toilet, when they eat, where and when they sleep.

The Oxford dictionary definition of dominance is:
'power and influence over others.'

I'm sure we can agree that we have power and influence over our dogs, we put a lead and collar on them, we choose what food they eat so with this in mind we don't need any 'dominance' training programs to reinforce this to our dogs. And we certainly do not need to use forceful methods such as pinning the dog down, hitting them nor scaring them.

If we look at people, some people naturally are leaders or influencers, and there are some who are never meant to fill this role, their upbringing, their experiences partly shape this but also somewhat influenced by their genes and their natural born character. Which although I have tried to categorize the following familiar characters in dogs as clearly as possible, think of it more as a general guide, as one tool of many to help you when forming or adding to your pack.

If you want a more comprehensive understanding of canine functional characters then please look up my good friend Dr Isla Fishburn or visit www.kachinacanine.com.

'Humans need to be calm, benevolent role models'

Not screaming banshees attempting the old school alpha domineering, overbearing characters.

Common Functional Characters

Leader

Despite popular belief, this dog can often appear a little reserved with new people. Sometimes very cunning (more so in bitches) and adept at problem solving. Often described as aloof, regal, snobby, standoffish and hesitant. Usually they remain toward the back of a litter or group when a potential threat is present, and can be keen on using a natural form of communication to control the movement of other group members, usually of the same gender. Calm and confident in nature when in their comfort zone. Often independent and less likely to suffer separation anxiety when young or an adult so long as they have a safe space within the home. Failing this they can become victims of separation anxiety if an only dog, where behaviour modification programmes have little to no effect. Frequently the last to be rehomed in a litter because of their natural reservation to move forward when presented to new people, environments, object etc. Highly intelligent, easy to train but is the type of dog who will 'switch off' after doing something a couple of times as it has gained the knowledge it needs and doesn't feel the need to repeat it if the teaching is not made more complicated.

Functions within a pack - holds all the knowledge for directing the group, keeps itself safe which is why it often lets the rest of the pack run ahead, or stays a little behind you…why?...because the bold and brash can get harmed if danger is out there first, while it remains safe.

Bitches - use speed and direction to control others, as they would when hunting prey, this often means they will test human females at certain times of the month, standing in their path, blocking doorways, etc.

Notes - always best to be with another dog when left without humans, the least likely to be influenced by the other dogs' behaviour issues, less management needed.
Sometimes after trauma recall can become an issue. Post-trauma this type of dog is more likely to bolt home when spooked on a walk.

Trust in the owner and their knowledge is everything, once this is lost it is tough to earn back again. Safety from a perceived threat is vital for this dog.

Enforcer

The nightclub bouncer, the one who follows the rules and ensures everyone else does too. The one who in past days of 'dominance theory' training was often mistaken as the 'alpha' or the bolshy one, often the first puppy to come to you out of the litter, the bravest. I have three of these myself, often these are the dogs that when you have more than one are the most likely to cause issues as they are predisposed to using strength, confidence or aggression when they feel it's necessary. Breed will come into the likelihood of this (i.e., a German Shepard or Rottweiler is bred for guarding/herding so more likely to be a problem than say a Cavalier King Charles whose sole purpose is to be a companion to mankind).

As a pet or family member, these dogs thrive off a consistent owner with consistent direction and guidance. Lack of boundaries and consistency often make this dog take on the associated character of Quality Control (which is explained next) and are likely to use force more often.

These dogs are often chosen to be working, or competition dogs. They are very intelligent and easy to train and enjoy performing tasks that can be repetitive. I haven't purposefully chosen to have three bitches of this character in my current pack, two of which are the same breed but it does come in handy as I enjoy training and competing with more than one dog.

These dogs are often real lead pullers and wander far away on off lead walks as it is their job to reach the boundaries, gain information and feed it back to the leader or owner. Also, it is the dog who is most likely to bark when the doorbell rings and want to get to the visitors first and investigate them, again this is their job, and while most dogs will do this, in a pack environment they will make sure they reach the visitor first.

Enforcers enforce the protocols and instructions they have been taught on others, so will tell other family/pack members off for not sticking to these.

Now it's worth noting that in certain breeds it's easy to mislabel all or most as the Enforcer, for example, if we look at the typical Labrador character – confident, bold often bolshy. This is the breed, and we need to assess all the little nuances between each dog to evaluate character correctly. What makes my current pack work with having three of such character is their age gaps, and the different roles they have within our family.

Quality Control

This dog isn't for the faint-hearted! Even the most experienced of trainers will struggle with this dog. I for one would never have one as my lifestyle fluctuates too much to meet its needs.

The dog who will test all members of the family, canine, feline and human. They will constantly be asking the question are you up to your 'job' today, is the pack or family effective and can we keep everyone safe. This character will test even the Leader, Enforcer and us. Other dogs will deal with this with a hard look, quick air snap or low grumble and if needed by appearing to put them to the floor (DO NOT try to create this in human-dog communication). Sometimes it appears at first glance that this dog is being bullied by all the other dogs, but if we watch them, they have instigated each interaction. Once the other dog has answered - 'Yes! Now leave me alone!' QC will move on and appear more settled in its demeanor after the interaction. Now it is not up to us to react in the same way when tested, we are not dogs, and dogs know that, us attempting to act like one is well pointless and often pathetic and untrustworthy in the dog's eyes. While this dog is at the best of times exasperating, frustrating and well plain annoying, the best thing we can do is take a deep breath, stay calm and ask them to do something such as sit, wait, down, etc. which re-enforces who and what we are in the family unit. This dog will push buttons and is not ever suitable to be the first family dog.

It is constantly questioning and wanting answers, noticing anything strange or different. Dislikes change and is suspicious. May mouth and nip, including heels and may be nervy jumpy and hyperactive, especially to sudden changes within the environment. Needs routine.

This dog thrives off a strict routine, while it has a routine and it is followed it will test less and less and become almost an easy dog. Any deviations from this routine and you will see the return of testing behaviours. Which can make holidays with your dog or day trips out if they are not the norm a less than enjoyable experience.
From a training perspective these dogs will learn new exercises pretty quickly and will have 'got it after just a handful of repetitions, repeating more than this will see the dog appear to 'lose it' in other words testing the rules - if I do this does it work, will I get the reward?

They have a very inquisitive nature, and if adding a second dog to an existing QC the best mix would be an Enforcer, so they have someone to follow.

Most people experiencing issues with their dog or with an adolescent dog will think they have a QC dog, this is rarely accurate, sometimes and associated character for specific situations or in the case of the 'teenager dog' a phase that will pass, consistency and staying calm is the key.

Follower

The easiest dog, easier than most other functional characters! What every dog owner who just wants an easy pet dog should have and advisable for a first time dog owner.

You could have 1, 2, 5 or even 10 of these and never have an issue of conflict between them. I have two of these and would happily have more.

They will be affable, biddable, adaptable, laid back, accepting of change and will deal with frustration well. Happy go lucky, they will be an ideal family dog.

Followers are as the title says, to follow the direction and instruction of others. In general, they are pretty laid back, will join in where there is fun, mischief or excitement to be had but kind of wait on the sidelines until then. They are the middle of the road type dog, neither very intelligent (which often can lead to trouble as they outwit us), nor brain dead. Relatively easy to train, very forgiving, a great character to have living with children. They can play the clown, but never in a nasty way. Happy to follow everyone else's lead.

Onlooker

A highly alert, on edge and often a very barky dog. Insecure I think is the best way to describe this dog. Its function is to alert the family to anything that may be happening. They hear a noise in the distance, bark, someone is wearing something they haven't seen before, bark, a strange vehicle in the distance, bark. You get the picture. Some breeds will naturally be more prone to barking than others, this must be considered when assessing. The barking is often followed by running away or hiding. They are literally there to tell us something that could potentially be a threat in the hope that the other dogs or we will go and deal with it often staying toward the back, and if in the presence of the leader, behind them. No confidence despite all the most careful socialization in the world. I often picture this dog as the typical small dog with an elderly person who barks from behind their legs.

This dog will be submissive, have low body posture and when scolded or corrected may urinate. He is nervy, vocal, anxious and may well suffer from separation anxiety. Will dislike new environments. Will be a barker at the slightest sound.

Less common characters

Provider

A dog who thrives off hunting and chasing, again breed traits will need to be taken into account.

For example because a working Cocker or a Beagle will be hard-wired to hunt this does not mean it is of Provider character. This character is very laid back, almost lazy at home. Calm and confident in the house or when on lead. Off lead on a mission. Likely to display the 'lay in wait then pounce' behaviour around their furry friends in a playful manner particularly on walks. Very intelligent, easy to train in all things other than when they are 'in hunting mode' to come back when called the first time. This character can be either gender, but often it can be seen more in a female than a male. I have a male provider myself, Moss. I often see litters of pups without any providers in it which is why I have categorised it as more of a rare character. This type of dog will be agile, quick. It will use speed, direction and have stamina and endurance.

Peacekeeper

If you have this, you are fortunate indeed! You have likely never needed help from a dog trainer. A Peacekeeper is a dog who will attempt to reduce conflict or calm the pack down in times of tension or overexcitement. They will either play the clown to distract the other dogs or us or physically put themselves between two dogs fighting (or us humans arguing, dancing or hugging). Highly intelligent, almost born wise. Very intuitive and a great comfort to humans in times of low mood. Very well respected and highly regarded by all members of the pack, including the leader. These are the best type of dog to have as a 'nanny dog' either to other dogs or children.

I have not seen two of these characters in the same pack, and because I wouldn't imagine any issues between them plus this is very unlikely to happen as they are such a rarity.

Solitary/Loner

I was slightly apprehensive of allowing this as an individual category. Please do not mistake this dog as a dog who should always live alone, they can live alongside others, but they are unlikely to form any meaningful bonds with other canine companions.

I have yet to see a true, born Loner. I'm not sure they exist. This is often due to circumstance or traumatic experience or lack of early socialisation with its own species under 8 weeks of age. A loner has no interest at all in interacting with other dogs, is happy with its person or people, aloof with other people. Not a hard dog to own.

A dog who lives alone is different from a Loner character. We have simply put the dog in a situation where it is the only one of its species in the household. A single dog will learn to play around with most of these characters, particularly the ones immediately below or above their natural born character and they often become very good at it. This will change depending on how we react to certain situations, and trauma will undoubtedly play a part in this. This is one of the reasons I decided to restrict this book to mainly introducing a puppy rather than an adult dog as most commonly it will be a rescue, where it's unlikely we will ever know for sure what trauma it may have experienced and how to assess its functional character correctly. Of course, it's possible to assess a rescue dog to be part of a pack, but that deserves its own literary title.
I believe we as humans are very similar, and we also change our character depending on what company or situation we are in.

Functional characters are not the be all and end all by any means but getting two dogs of the same character without considering other factors can end in disaster. I do have three Enforcers in my house, but there is a way to do it! (The 'formulas for a happy pack' chapter will help explain).

9
Associated characters

How experience and our behaviour affect functional characters

'Knowledge is power'

Or should I say knowledge creates influence? Every time a dog sniffs at something it's analyzing the data and gaining knowledge, though it doesn't make a Beagle who is bred to trail scents more intelligent than another breed that isn't. Dogs always want more information, after all, they have to live in our strange human world with our ever-changing moods and routines. Dogs love to learn, which is why we can train them, we are giving them information. An experienced and knowledgeable dog is often calm confident and highly regarded amongst other dogs as it can influence other dogs in how to behave when strange things happen. If we are calm and collected the first time a banger goes off in the distance with our dog, our dog is more likely to look to us for guidance, we influence them by showing them we are not bothered, so they do not need to be. The first couple of times the dog may jump or wince but then with enough repetition most dogs (having never before heard a similar noise) will relax.

My own boy Merlin is as bomb proof as they come, although a Follower, he is true to his breed being bold and confident (somewhat similar to a Labrador in temperament), despite his years he is still quite puppyish in his behaviour in certain situations, but again this is true to his breed. The flat-coat retriever is what is described as the 'Peter Pan of the dog world' they never grow up and are very clownish.
Being big black and fluffy he has been invaluable over the years helping me to rehabilitate countless dogs who are either insecure or aggressive

toward other dogs. Being black other dogs will struggle to read his face and body language as it's in shadow, this then will often bring the worst out in other dogs. He has learned through careful management by me and lots of repetition what signals to give, or not give in some cases to each dog, down to the most minute detail to help the other dogs feel at ease and that he is no threat. He is the dog that any visiting dog will always curl up with. He is an expert at helping me raise puppies and also helping calm down bouncy pushy adolescent dogs too.

This kind of thing is so very rare to see in any dog nowadays, and I am so fortunate to have him. Remember he is a Follower….so on paper, he should not really have all of these qualities and be so very fluent in the intricacies of dog language, but he is. Why? Because he has gained knowledge and experience by being in these situations over and over for many years. Because he holds this knowledge other dogs who may be of a higher character will respect him and sometimes seek his company (or I like to think of it as seeking his counsel like you would an elder). Once he has gained the trust of these dogs that I work with I can then introduce a third dog, and Merlin will influence the client's dog into believing this new dog is safe. His breed and also his born character also lend him to being a big softy. I have yet to find something, animal, dog or human that he would growl at, that's not to say it won't happen, but he is now ten years of age. Moss is the highest male in our pack, yet he regularly seeks Merlin's company and finds comfort in being around him, 90% of their sleeping time is spent curled up together.

Trauma and associated characters

What do I mean by an 'associated character'? I mean a dog who for example is naturally a born Follower character and who has learned to display certain QC traits and perform the traits pretty well. In this example the associated character is QC. When this happens, it's often due to an adverse experience they have had (AKA trauma) which has unbalanced their view of the world to the extent that they feel they have to change to compensate or cope with the world, for fear of the trauma happening again. Usually associated characters are the position above or below what their natural character is. So an enforcer character will take on a leader or QC character, in some cases, they may display both characters above and below depending on the situation they are in. This is why having rescue dogs and introducing them into an established pack can be a minefield. Until you have spent lots of time with them and introduced them to many other dogs who you are confident of their character and assessed how they interact, you won't be sure of their true character. This is because of the possibility of many different trauma experiences. This has made the rescue dog so well practiced at an associated position.

10
Sex, seasons, neutering and breeding

Sex and neutering

The role of male canids – to protect
The role of bitch canids – to provide

The above is a very general sweeping statement and in my experience, more relevant to wolves than our domestic canine, but the more dogs we have, the more you will see these qualities come to the surface.

Neutering makes a female dog smell and sometimes act like a male dog 80% of the time and vice versa with a male dog. This should be taken into account in all multi-dog situations.

A bitch who is spayed at the wrong point in her cycle (i.e., not at the midpoint between seasons) can cause her to be of real interest to male dogs, mainly intact males for the rest of her life. This is because she will be perceived by others to be still entire and at that point in her cycle that she was spayed. For example, it's a little-known fact that for nine weeks after a season they secrete all the same pheromones as if they were pregnant even if they were not mated, or even if they are suffering a phantom pregnancy or not as the case may be.

Best practice when neutering contrary to many vets advice is to wait until your dog is fully grown and mature. This is usually at around the 12-18 months mark for small to medium dogs and 18 months to 2 years for large dogs such as Labradors or over two years for giant breeds such as great Danes or St Bernards. Neutering before sexual and physical maturity can have side effects such as joint and bone issues. Hormones help our dogs to physically and mentally develop so removing these at a young age will affect their ability to mature into the calm adult dogs we want to live with.

It's always worth checking with your breed club or breed council if you have a pedigree breed as to what the latest recommendations are with regards to best age for spay or neuter.

There are many pros and cons to neutering, and with a multi-dog household with different sexes, it is something that is often considered early on if we are not planning to breed.

If you are planning to breed any of your pack, whether together or using your boy as a stud dog or taking your bitch to a stud dog for mating and then raising the litter at home there are additional factors to consider....particularly if you are breeding from your bitch. I am not talking about caring for the puppies here, again that's not what this book is about, though it is likely to be a part of my next book.

A brood bitch in a multi-dog household

If you have more than one bitch, the ideal scenario should be that you are breeding from your higher character bitch. Why? Because this would be how a wild pack would work and if breeding from your lower ranking bitch you should expect the higher bitch to have something to say about it, particularly if both are entire and at a fertile age. In some cases the decision to breed from your lower ranking bitch may prove a fatal error as the higher will not approve. They see it as their right to reproduce as they are more knowledgeable. I have seen it time and time again when the higher bitch will forever then 'pick on', the lower ranking bitch as if to assert her authority at the injustice of a litter produced that she was not entitled to have.

Using your male dog as a stud dog will increase his testosterone levels for four months after each mating, this makes them more assertive and likely to use force against other pack members if they feel it is needed.

I often see multi-dog households with numerous entire bitches all within the breeding age bracket, with the higher ranking bitches suppressing the lower ranking bitches seasons which can be problematic on multiple levels. Often in such multi-dog households the bitches have a history of fights and the owner has put some management protocols in place, such as keeping bitches separate from others.

The first season

The first season of a bitch can also alter the dynamics of the pack, mainly if you have older entire bitches. This is the time when your young bitch is reaching sexual maturity, and there may be some altercations between the bitches during this time, this although normal (within reason, depending on the extent of the disputes) it's a distressing time for humans and for the bitches in question. Where possible treat the older bitch with preference and priority, more treats, chews, general perks to help minimise any potential issues. If a fight occurs, keep the bitches separated until the season is over and then introduce again through walks and gradually reintegrate them post season. If you are unsure on any of this, please call in a professional. This is a hard subject to advise on specifically, as each dynamic is different.

If you have an entire male (or more than one intact male) and your pup is a bitch, when they have their first season it will also be distressing for the males, and they should be kept separate from the young bitch for the whole of the season. I prefer to send Moss to a friend when I have a bitch in season as this is the least distressing all around. Entire males who can smell a bitch in season in the home can become vocal, destructive and refuse to eat which is understandably also distressing for us humans.

First seasons are usually somewhere between 6 &12 months of age and last for three weeks, BUT and I mean, BUT I have known bitches have their first seasons for just five days, for six weeks and can start at ages five months and as late as twenty one months.

Some breeds will only have a season once a year, but most dogs will have a season every 6 months. Ripple's grandmother went 8 months between seasons while Fern (pre-spaying) was a 7 month bitch. Ripples first season was at 6 months and lasted 2 and a half weeks. Time will tell how long between seasons as she hasn't yet had her second.

Every dog is different.....change the record I can hear you saying! Every dog really is different, there's always an average, and we can bracket and quantify and label to our heart's content to give you an overview, but there is always going to be that one, the one we can't label, quantify or put in a bracket or category.

First seasons are a real milestone for a young bitch, not only are they reaching sexual maturity, mentally they are not mature, yet their body is changing, other dogs change in their intention and communication toward them, and nothing is what it once was to them. Some youngsters will cope very well, and you will only notice by the amount they are cleaning their lady parts, others will appear depressed and lethargic. A transitional period, so a change in behaviour is expected, above all protect your bitch, and keep their mind occupied with toys, games, treat dispensing toys and chews. My advice for a first season is to not walk them at all during this time as you don't know when her most fertile time (i.e., when they will accept a mating from a dog) will be, as you don't know how long the first season will be.

Usually after the first season a bitch will have a 'normal' 21 day season and be fertile after 10 days for up to a week, in which case I will only walk them on lead, away from other dogs for the first ten days and then not walk them until I am confident they are out of season.

11
Formulas for a happy pack

If you have all Follower dogs and plan to get another, none of the following applies.

If, however, you want something a little different to a Follower this time around, keep reading.

Stay with me as this may give you a little brain strain before you get your head around it.

The rule of four

The formula to ensure a harmonious group of dogs. You need to apply each of the following rules to each pair of dogs, the more differences between each two dogs, the better!
1. Age – minimum of four years age gap.
2. Sex – opposite sex is best (refer to previous chapter for a reminder on how neutering can affect this).
3. Breed – different breed or breed type.
4. Character – different functional character, the exception to this rule is if you have multiple Follower dogs. You could have 10 of these and not have an issue.

The Follower character is what most people want and are the easiest to deal with. If you want one for competition, working, etc. maybe a higher-ranking pup would be a better fit (though these jobs are still possible for a Follower).

Apart from getting two high or low dogs, another thing to avoid would be a highest and lowest (with no dogs in the middle) as these may prove hard work.

The best practice for just two dogs to get along, living together is if you follow the rule of four to the letter. This way you can be confident of no issues between the two dogs.

More than two dogs and it gets more complex.

Example of my current pack –

Dog	Breed	Sex / Neutered	Functional Character	Age Now
Merlin	Flatcoat Retriever	M/Yes	Follower	10 years
Moss	Mini L/H Dach	M/No (stud dog)	Provider	7 years
Mica	Springer Spaniel	F/Yes	Enforcer	11 years
Ziggy	Mini L/H Dach	M/Yes	Follower	12 years
Fern	Mini L/H Dach	F/Yes	Enforcer	5 years
Ripple	Mini L/H Dach	F/No	Enforcer	10 months

Best practice is **4 out of 4** (100% Success rate for the dogs to cohabit amicably)– for example, if we look at Merlin and Fern

Merlin is five years older than Fern (minimum four-year age gap)
They are totally different breeds
They are opposing sexes and both neutered.
Fern is an Enforcer and Merlin is a Follower.
This is 100% the best practice and no issues.

They aren't bosom buddies, they don't choose to curl up together much, but they do get on well.

They do not need to be best friends, as dogs like us have favorites or besties but we also have good friends who we enjoy spending time with.

Merlin and Fern are pair of dogs that together they tick all of the four boxes, which means we can be confident in their compatibility.

Let's look at a **3 out of 4** mix (75% of the time the dogs will get on. This is not to say the dogs will fight 25% of the time, but they may not see eye to eye some of the time).

Merlin and Mica

Points for-
Different breeds
Opposing sexes (and both neutered)
Different functional characters

Against –
Only one year age gap (this should be four years or more to be a positive).

The three points that are in favour of a harmonious relationship between the two dogs are their differing breeds, sexes (both neutered) and their functional characters.
Their one-year age gap does go against them, this is the 25% as described above, this puts them in potential competition with each other some of the time.
Because of this formula you can expect them to be great 75% of the time, I would say it's a little more than this, they get on well and being the largest two in size of the pack are often walked, travelled and exercised together. The only very mild conflict comes when both are chasing a ball or toy, and even then it's more in a playful 'look what I got, and I know you want it' way from Merlin to Mica. Mica does her typical 'I'll lunge at you and possibly show my teeth to show my disapproval', but Merlin's playful character feeds off this and carries on playing the annoying little brother role. That's the worse it ever gets! I am very fortunate as not all three out of four mixes work as well as this, but I have yet to see this mix where it has caused real issues.

2 out of 4 mix (50% - the dogs have potential to get on with each other ok for half of the time, leaving a high percentage of risk of this mix becoming sour toward one another).

Fern and Ripple

Points for –
Age gap (4.5years)
Sex (we can count these as being the opposite sex despite both being bitches, Fern is spayed so smells and acts like a male enforcer 80% of the time)

Against –

Same Breed
Same Character

Now really, they should only get on 50% of the time, and I know if I didn't spend the amount of time separately with them that I do it would be closer to this figure. Ripple and Fern spend large amounts of time with us and doing different activities, this tips the scales in our favour. These two dogs get on well, occasionally choose to play with each other and sometimes cuddle up together.

I have seen these mixes cause issues when not managed appropriately. More commonly when both dogs are of the same sex either both neutered or both entire. But still, this is the minority in multidog household problems that I encounter.

1 out 4 mix (25% chance of the dogs getting along).
Personally, I do not ever have any dogs in my pack that are of this mix, and I do this on purpose as this is not advisable, so I will make up an example for you

Dog A – Female/entire 4-year-old small terrier QC
Dog B – Female/entire 4-year-old small terrier Enforcer

Points for –
Different Characters

Against –
Same age
Same sex
Same breed or breed type

I have seen these mixes work, but rarely. The Enforcer bitch will usually naturally take the slight upper hand here, but this can be arduous work and often ends in options 1, 2 or 3 being put into action (as described in chapter 2).

Worst case –
0 out of 4 mix (0% chance of this working for any length of time in a household without serious intervention and management)
Personally, I do not ever have any dogs in my pack that are of this mix, and I do this on purpose as this is guaranteed to end in heartache

Dog A – male/neutered 4-year-old small terrier Enforcer

Dog B – male/neutered 4-year-old small terrier Enforcer
This can sometimes be two dogs from the same litter

Points for –
Nothing goes in their favour

Against –
Same sex
Same character
Same age
Same breed/type

Now some dogs of this mix will tolerate being in each other's company, and if you watch them closely they almost ignore the other's existence, usually though this is from chance encounters with friends dogs or dogs on the park. Two living together is another story. It's all about competition, and they are virtually identical despite the fact they may be different in colour or pattern.

More often fights occur on a regular basis and sometimes result in severe injuries and or death.

The most crucial factor in this equation is the fact that both dogs are hard-wired to enforce the rules so are more prone to showing aggressive behavior when they feel it is needed to back up their wishes. Also, the fact that they are both terriers so are hard-wired to chase, bite, kill small vermin, but can easily transfer these skills when in a fight for what they perceive is their survival. The better mix would be if they were both numbers. If they were both onlookers, they would get on ok but would make our life as humans a misery, not to mention feed off each other's constant alert and insecure energies, so not advisable. In a nutshell, just don't do it. Plus, a little reminder about not getting two dogs at once.

Notes about my pack - All dogs bar Ripple (youngest) are highly experienced at helping me with client's dogs, they are stooge dogs, and I use them for teaching. They all have lots of knowledge to share, and apart from Fern they are all confident dogs able to take on other roles/characters when required. This comes from years of working with me in a professional capacity, traveling up and down the country with me, competing, doing displays and been in countless environments, all of which help with their ability to adapt when needed.

Not all of my mixes are ideal on paper, but all get on well, some play with certain pack members or choose to share beds with more than they will with others, can you guess which?

Multiple dogs and ensuring a happy pack is my specialty, my passion. It's because of this I do push the boundaries a little with my own pack, I am confident in my ability to manage certain characters and I also take into account my lifestyle. If you aren't confident in this, stick to the 4 out of 4 rule and you won't go wrong.

Fighting and gender

Two bitches fighting is often worse than two dogs…and I think it's the same for humans! Two bitches are more likely to 'hold a grudge' and to do more damage to each other.
Two dogs fighting (except if they are fighting over breeding rights/ a bitch in season) is rarely as severe as two bitches, this is not to say you should just ignore them, some dogs will 'hold grudges' but this is more likely with entire males than neutered as they are hormone driven also.

It is uncommon to have dogs and bitches fighting, particularly if both are entire - but it does happen. I have yet to experience or hear of a dog, and bitch fight (in a multidog household) where there wasn't something else involved such as guarding a resource such as food or a toy, etc.

12
How to choose the breeder, what to look for, and what to ask

Write down any questions you have before you visit the breeder. It's likely that you will forget them while you are there.

Take an experienced trainer or behaviourist or a good breeder with you. They won't be emotionally involved and will be able to give you good advice.

Best practice when finding a breeder

DO

Ask to see the puppy's mother, which should be present. This is VERY important. The temperament of the puppy mainly comes from the mother. If you don't like the mother's personality, don't buy a pup.

See the puppy in the environment it was bred in; the best setting is the FAMILY HOME. If you suspect that the conditions are not right, DO NOT BUY THE PUPPY.

Be prepared to be put on the breeder's waiting list - a healthy puppy is worth waiting for.
Ask if you can return the puppy if things don't work out; a responsible and reputable breeder will always say yes.

Be suspicious of a breeder selling more than one (maximum two) breeds, unless you are sure of their credentials.

Try to go to a Kennel Club Assured breeder or at least a breeder who register their pups with the Kennel Club if you are buying a pedigree dog - while this is no guarantee of a healthy animal, nor any guarantee that they are not a puppy farmer it does weed out the majority.

Ask if the pups and parents have had any relevant health tests AND ASK TO SEE THE RESULTS.

Ask the breeder as many questions as you can. If they are a responsible breeder, they will be pleased to answer them.

Why did they choose to breed their bitch in the first place?

Ask what the breeding was designed to achieve, why the stud was selected for example.

A litter should be bred for a reason. Not only to produce puppies for sale.

What activities do they do with their dogs? Most reputable breeders will compete in some way with their dogs, whether that is showing them or working them.

If possible, ask for contact with a previous buyer from the breeder in order to see a pup from a previous litter.

Ask what socialisation has been done, e.g. car rides, meeting people, busy places, vehicles, noises. A new owner should expect a pup to be able to slot into modern life.

What back up does the breeder provide? If there are problems, is the breeder willing to help either by phone or by visits?

Does the breeder want to stay in touch with you and the pup? If not then why not?

Do they provide advice regarding feeding? Will the new puppy come with some food and instructions about nutrition?

Will I get a certificate showing the worming dates for my puppy?

If I take my pup to my vet for a health check and my vet finds something wrong do I get a full refund on the puppy?

Will the dog come with four weeks insurance?

Will my puppy be microchipped? It is now a legal requirement that the breeder needs to microchip puppies before leaving.

Be prepared to answer lots of questions from the breeder! They should be interviewing YOUR suitability to have one of their pups!

Do you feel like they are interrogating you? If you do, this is an excellent sign.

DON'T

Don't buy a puppy from a pet shop – they have often come from puppy farms.

Don't pick your puppy up from a 'neutral location' such as a motorway service station. This is a common tactic used by puppy farmers.

Don't buy a puppy because it is in terrible conditions and you feel sorry for it. It is hard to walk away, but if you buy the puppy, you are perpetuating the problem (and making space for another poor puppy). Leave and report the breeder.

Don't be fooled by a Kennel Club certificate; they are often faked by puppy farmers who are operating illegally and have no qualms about falsifying paperwork. The majority of puppy farmers will not register their litters with the Kennel Club. If in doubt check with the Kennel Club.

www.mykc.org.uk is a wonderful tool to use to check pedigrees, to check if your pup has been registered and of any health tests of the parents. You only need to ask for the bitch/mother of pup's registered name (as long as she is registered with the UK Kennel Club) for you to check more details through this website.

Don't be persuaded by the breeder to have two puppies from the same litter or different litters. It is NOT better to have two puppies together.

Don't buy a puppy with any obvious health issue.

Don't buy a puppy over ten weeks of age. The cut-off point for socialisation is 12-16 weeks.

What to look for in a breeder/puppy when looking for a companion dog

Puppies should be reared in the house – not in a garage/kennel/shed, etc.

Never take home an only pup (only one survived, only one born) unless you are very experienced, if you do, expect to have frustration issues to deal with.

Ideal litter size is 5 for a well-rounded/temperament puppy (but not a crucial point).

The mother of the pups shows no signs of illness, distress or spooking.

The mother should be seen with the pups (not in a separate room to the puppies).

The breeder should have carried out relevant health checks for the breed on both father and mother – this includes health checks for both parents of designer or mixed breeds, etc.

The breeder should ask you about your lifestyle, work hours, intentions for the pup, etc.

The breeder should be able to tell you all about the breed but also should be asking you how much you know about the breed.

Never take the last pup if you have only seen that puppy and not seen it with its littermates.

Try and view the pups before they are old enough to go to new homes, giving you a chance to avoid the temptation of those puppy eyes pleading you to take them home the same day despite many things that may not tick boxes above and below.

It is crucial to have plenty of toys in with the litter at all times.

It is also important that at feeding times there are plenty more bowls than puppies (to reduce the chances of food aggression/guarding when they are older).

The puppies should have two separate surfaces in their pen/area this helps with toilet training to distinguish between places to toilet and sleep/play/eat

The breeder should offer advice for the lifetime of the dog.

The breeder should not have more than four separate breeds.

If the breeder is breeding more than three litters per year, they should have a licence for some local councils.

A breeder ideally should breed no more than two litters per year if that.

Pups should be weaned onto a wide range of different foods to avoid allergies, and puppies should never be weaned onto just one complete diet.

The mother of the puppies can separate herself from the puppies as and when she pleases (even if it is a shelf above the puppies) – not just kept away from them from weaning age, she should still be around the pups to discipline them, etc. up until the time they are ready to leave.

The breeder should be able to tell you of all the places they have taken the pups, i.e., in the car, the vets, the garden and also how many different types of people the puppies have met, young, old, with hats, without, glasses, sticks, different races of people, etc.

The breeder who only offers you a pup on breeding terms should also be avoided. Breeding terms would be something like asking to have the bitch or dog back in future to breed from, or that you breed from them and once they have a puppy back from you they will register your pup (now an adult dog) in your name, the registration stays with the breeder until this time. Often these arrangements involve a lower initial purchase price which can be tempting but the arrangement rarely works well in practice.

The breeder can tell you about the different personalities of the pups and advise on which may suit you best.

13
Choosing the puppy – identifying the individual within a litter

Within the litter, how do we tell who is what character?

I would always advise to go and view the litter between 3 & 5 weeks and again around 6-8 weeks before making a final choice.

Refer back to the Functional characters chapter for more in-depth, but the primary qualities in each puppy/character are as follows -

Leader - stays in the nest or runs back to it when visitors arrive, reserved, aloof, has its own agenda. Has a regal presence.
Enforcer - the first one to greet you, confident, inquisitive, bolshy, often the biggest, chunkiest boldest pup (what most people describe as the one who chose them).
QC - rushes out to greet you then quickly runs back, slightly nervy, jumpy and nippy.
Follower - friendly, middle of the pups, happily be placed in any position, happy to be held in your arms belly up. Easy going, very accepting.
Onlooker - runs and hides behind mother, nervous, skittish.
Provider - chilled out, calm as a cucumber, the best way to test for this character, get a feather or similar on a string and move it quickly, most of the pups will be interested and start to chase. A Provider will carry on pursuing after all other puppies give up. Happy to sleep away from the other puppies, reasonably independent. May be seen 'pouncing' on littermates more than the others.

Peacekeeper - wise beyond its weeks, self-assured, the clown, will place its self between other pups squabbling.

If you are unsure, video the pups playing, with you, with toys and with each other, drop your car keys or something similar near the litter (so it makes a strange noise) and watch how they react, who bounces back the quickest? Who avoids the keys or that area for a good while after? This way you can watch and analyse over and over at home.

If you are lucky enough to visit the litter when they are under three weeks of age, and still feeding from mum, take note of who is nearest the mother's back end, where do they feed on the milk bar? The richest in nutrient teats are the furthest to the rear of the bitch, so you will often find leader/enforcer feeding at that end with the Follower and Onlooker at the teats closer to the bitches chest. I must add though if the breeder interferes and places pups on teats, this will not show an accurate idea of position.

To pick the right puppy from the litter on character, it takes a few visits and some supporting information from the breeder, you need to build a picture of each pup and piece together the evidence.

If you have one dog and are looking to get a second the rules for this should be pretty clear for you using the formula/rule of four.

If however, you have more, this is where it gets a little tricky.

Let's have a look at my pack again and try to see what kind of dog would fit if I were going to get puppy number 7...

Dog	Breed	Sex / Neutered	Natural/Associated	Age Now
Merlin	Flatcoat Retriever	M/Yes	Follower/higher	10 years
Moss	Mini L/H Dach	M/No (stud dog)	Provider/Leader	7 years
Mica	Springer Spaniel	F/Yes	Enforcer/Loner	11 years
Ziggy	Mini L/H Dach	M/Yes	Follower/Onlooker	12 years
Fern	Mini L/H Dach	F/Yes	Enforcer/QC	5 years
Ripple	Mini L/H Dach	F/No	Enforcer/Peacekeeper	10 months

Follower would work, dog or bitch, any breed and even though it would be close in age to Ripple it wouldn't cause an issue if the play was managed well. The joy in having a Follower dog!
I could also have a Leader, a bitch would be better than a dog to eliminate the risk of conflict with Moss. There are quite a few options, but I will not be going above six dogs, I have had seven for a short

while and its wasn't pleasurable for me. Others can and do cope very well with seven or more but we are all different.

The breed or mix of breeds is highly relevant. As I have said before, terriers are hardwired to chase, bite and kill small vermin, so are more likely to uses these skills to protect themselves. Same for guarding breeds, they have guarding instincts and are hardwired to be wary of strangers of all species and will defend themselves when/if needed. Gundogs have been bred for many years to work alongside other dogs and people so are in my experience the most sociable group toward other dogs and people. This has been selected for over many generations so you may be able to get away with not following the rule of four so closely....but is it worth the risk of being the exception to the rule? Despite all the help and advice, I offer in this book, there is always and I mean always the exception to the rule....so eyes and ears open, watch your pack, watch them interact and keep the balance.

I have an equal split of dogs and bitches (neutered and entire), so it really wouldn't matter what sex I would get next, but my preference would be a dog because, well, I prefer them, but that really is down to personal preference.

14
To play or not to play that is the question

Humans playing with dogs with toys and food? Yes, yes, yes! Don't forget it's so important that we bond with our dogs more than they bond with each other.

Letting them play with each other? Hmm, not a great idea on the whole.

Do my dogs play with each other? Yes
Do they play all the time? No
Do they play every day? No
Do I have to micromanage this? As adults no, but I put the work in when they were young.

On the flip side, play is useful in small doses between dogs but only in small, supervised and managed sessions.

If you let your pup play with your adult dog or dogs continually it can and in most cases will cause an issue. As humans we can tire of having a human toddler around, our patience starts to wain as the hours progress, and we feel great relief when they either have a nap, go to bed, or they go home if they aren't ours.

Consider your adult dog, having a puppy trying to play continuously, hanging off their ears and tails isn't fun. Some dogs will move away, get somewhere out of reach of the pup if we don't intervene (in my opinion this is the best case scenario when we don't intervene first, which is why it's essential the adult dogs can escape if needs be). Others will either put up with it (and look to us for help) or floor the puppy, telling it off. While most may feel this is natural and in some cases, I myself do allow this to happen but only with dogs who I know will just use the minimum force necessary to reprimand puppy (usually a growl and an air snap. No physical contact). Many dogs will go overboard with their use of reprimand and really scare the puppy which can affect their confidence in future interactions with other dogs. The last category of dog tries to appease the puppy by playing and playing and playing. Usually, this is either a mature older Follower dog or a dog that is less than four years older than the pup. This bonds the two dogs together, to the point of them relying on each other too much which can then cause problems when you ask things of them such as recall from the garden or on walks.

Don't forget those puppy teeth are needle sharp! It is easy for us to snap at someone for catching us in the wrong spot when it hurts, and how do puppies explore the world? By putting things in their mouths.

From a health and development perspective play can cause real damage to your puppy's growing form. An injury is so easy at a young age as their skeleton is so soft, almost like jelly. Differences in size and weight between puppy and adult dog needs to be a real factor for consideration here.

Before Ripple arrived, I assessed my pack, where they were at in their life stages, functional characters, individual sociability and their patience with puppies and predicted who would be more or less tolerant of her at such a young age. From this I made an action plan, admittedly it was only in my head, but if I had of put it down on paper it would have looked something like this ;

Ziggy - well practiced with puppies, playful, very tolerant, has been known to tell the odd puppy off if they jump on his back, but only with vocalisations and body language, never making contact with his teeth. Being the oldest, he has been present for three litters of puppies raised in the house, plus he has helped raise Jazz (Ripple's Grandma), Merlin, Moss and Fern. He knows the routine of a new dog joining the family, and has helped with countless puppies as part of my work.

Action plan - because he is so well rounded and a happy chappy in almost every situation, bonding with Ziggy wouldn't be such a bad thing, but being careful not to let them bond too much, I will allow some play but in very short doses. Ziggy is also the lightest (weight wise) of the whole pack least likely to cause injury to Ripple's tiny and fragile frame.

Mica - aloof, not bothered by puppies (or dogs in general really). Is a dog who will naturally choose to move away if annoyed or disturbed, but if cornered will reprimand a puppy, more than I would like. Mica will bare teeth, air snap, not give many signals to the dog before resorting to this, she has never made contact with teeth but uses all her weight and body language to reinforce her point. This behaviour could scare some more sensitive puppies. Has experienced two litters being raised in the household, and been present for Moss and Fern joining the gang from puppies. The only dog I have ever known her to play with is Fern (which was a pleasant surprise when it first happened, it still happens but maybe once a month for just a few minutes) so I'm not overly worried about Ripple 'over bonding' to her. It's not out of the question that they may play at some point but unlikely and if it does, it won't be often enough to cause an issue.

Action Plan - always ensure Mica has somewhere to escape, most likely a chair or sofa. Be mindful of small spaces when the pup is with her.

Merlin - playful, patient, has never reprimanded nor even growled at a pup and is the type of dog to tolerate a puppy hanging off his tail and look to me for help. Has been present for three litters plus Moss and Fern. Not aware of his size or where his feet are, possible danger of accidental injury to pup at times such as visitors or us arriving in his excitement.

Action plan - initial introduction on lead to help minimise the risk of him standing on Ripple, likely have a lead on for first few times/days when Ripple is loose with Merlin (and always supervised). Be mindful of humans arriving when they are together or in times of excitement to protect Ripple from injury.

Moss - aloof, not tolerant of rude puppies who walk all over him or attempt to jump on him, very similar to Mica. Can/will guard items sometimes from other pack members but only by using vocalisations and body language. Puppies who give him due respect he will occasionally play with but takes a few days for him to do this. He has not been present for any litters raised in the house (he was one of the pups in my last litter), but he has been present for Fern's arrival, being a bitch he took to her reasonably quickly but I did do all the things I have said in this book to ensure success when Fern arrived.

Action Plan - not much other than to remember although he is Ripple's Dad this doesn't automatically bond them together, to limit play and to wait till pup is over six months before being loose with the whole pack when being fed high-quality things such as raw bones.

Fern - a rush in and tell them off first ask questions later type of girl. She was our last pup, so she hasn't been present for any other additions to the family. She is however quite playful with young dogs including puppies once she gets to know them (2-3 days) - one to manage and watch that she doesn't scare Ripple nor teach her this behaviour on greeting. She's a 'Daddies princess' and likely to object to any attention to Ripple from Mark.

Action plan - initial greeting on lead, treats to hand to reinforce the 'look, look back' (look at the pup, look at me, look at the pup, look at me, etc.) that I have taught to counteract her reactivity from a young age. Be mindful of Fern's needs for reassurance, particularly from my husband, Mark. Fern has a few behaviours that I am confident I do not want Ripple to learn. Lots of management needed for at least the first year of Ripple's life. Being the next youngest of the pack Ripple is likely to try and emulate her behaviours most and in time Fern will want to play often with her, this will be carefully managed. Some play will be allowed as it is crucial that Fern accepts Ripple and this will help with the process but in very short doses and not on a daily basis.

15

Before puppy comes home – smells, setups, placements of pen, preparation, a routine for existing dogs, feeding

It's quite a traumatic experience for any puppy when they leave their littermates, mum, breeder and home environment.

I have what is called a 'snuggle pup' it's a soft toy that looks like a dog, it has a velcro pocket underneath for a fake heartbeat (the feel of the pulse when you touch it or rest on it), and you can also put heat packs in there too. This helps to replicate the feeling of sleeping with her littermates and mum. Puppies like to pile on top of each other and sleep in a heap so I have made her crate very dark (with a blanket over) and cozy with the snuggle pup in there too. If I didn't have a snuggle pup, the best thing to use would be a hot water bottle (wrapped in a blanket or similar) and a ticking clock or watch wrapped up too for the heartbeat feel. When I collect Ripple, her breeder will provide me with a blanket that smells of her litter mates and mum which I will then place in her crate with her which will be the final touch.

Shopping list

- Barriers such as a pen, crate, baby gates, etc.
- A heat mat or similar -

- Snuggle safe heat pad
- Hot water bottle wrapped in a towel or blanket
- Electric heat mat for dogs/animals
- Copious amounts of chews and activities for your existing dog or dogs
- Bedding, towels, grooming puppy brushes, toys, chews, etc.
- Travel/car crates etc.
- Puppy pads if required
- Collar, tag, harness and lead
- A new diary or notebook to put all your plans, goals, achievements, struggles and activities in for you to refer to.
- Plenty of memory on your camera/phone for all the lovely cute pictures you will be taking
- Ear plugs, energy (caffeine in my case), patience, maybe your alcoholic beverage of choice and a sense of humour!

Just a little reminder that any behaviour or training concerns with existing furry family members should be tackled or at the very least started way before new puppy comes home

Puppy needs to have its own area, separate from the other dogs, and this could be a pen, crate or room. I usually use a puppy pen with the crate in it, in the area that my other dogs are in the day, which is the kitchen/conservatory/lounge (its open plan). If you are using another room, a baby gate or dog gate may be worth the investment to avoid shutting them out altogether. The aim is that puppy and dogs can interact but through a barrier when you are not around, provided the adult dogs are not growling or intimidating puppy through the barrier. Their separate area or pen in my case should be set up at least four weeks before puppy arrives. This allows the dogs to acclimatize to something new being there. This is even more important if you have elderly dogs who may have some sight loss so they can learn to navigate around it before being faced with a little bundle of fluff and teeth as well.

Put toys, bedding, puppy pads (if you plan to use them) anything you think puppy will have in the pen or area well in advance, again, so the dogs get used to this, I would even put a chew or such like in the pen regularly, so the dogs get used to the fact that good and exciting things are in there, but they do not get to have them. If you find your dogs are getting frustrated at something being in there, give them a chew at the same time you place anything food related into the pen or puppy area, you should only need to do this a few times before the dogs start to ignore the items they can't get to.

This will also be a test if you have large or athletic breeds as to whether they can get themselves into the pen! If they can, change it, make it higher, do whatever you can to make sure this does not happen. Puppy needs to feel safe in its area.

The area should be big enough or have the potential to be expanded to fit your puppy in when it is fully grown.

The puppy area is likely to be in place until the puppy is at least 6-8 months of age, more likely up to the age of 12 months so this is essential.

Ideally, you should have viewed the litter of puppies between the ages of 3 & 6 weeks as discussed previously. On this visit, please take a clean towel, blanket or such like and rub it all over the puppies, or if the breeder and bitch allow, put it in their sleeping area for a while so they can all sleep on it. Once it has the scent on bring it home and let your dogs smell it, leave it down so they can sleep on it, rest on it, play with it, in other words, do what they like with it. Try not to place this in just one dog's bed, if you have 'fixed beds' for each dog. I usually visit any new pup on a weekly basis so will do this every visit.

Dogs gain so much knowledge from a scent, and this exercise aims to acclimatize the dogs to the smell of another dog in the house, to the point that when the pup comes home, it's almost like greeting an old friend as their scent has been around well before the actual puppy. Of course, you will be bringing the smell of the puppies home on you, but I'm sure you also carry the scent of other dogs home on you regularly when you have met a dog out and about or at a friend's house, etc. so this is why we make it different. In human terms, if we have a friend who is always telling us how lovely their friend is and has done for a long time when we finally meet this person we have a favorable view of them and are more relaxed with them than if we just met them with no background information.

You can also do this the other way around, but only with permission of the breeder as some may be concerned about contagious diseases with such young immune systems which is fine. Our clothes will carry the scent our pack or dog when you are interacting with the litter. This can be in the form of giving toys to the breeder (new ones that you have rubbed over your dogs) or a blanket or towel for the bedding area and leaving it with the litter.

At least four weeks before pup comes home I would provide your existing dog or dogs with more toys, more regular chews (with multiple dogs I always offer more toys/chews than there are dogs to help prevent the need for them to guard these things). I would also be regularly separating myself from the dogs, behind a barrier (you will need to do this when training your puppy). This could be as simple as watching tv with the dogs in another area behind a baby gate or having them behind a barrier when you're cooking, cleaning, etc. I tend to find the dogs relax more if they can see us, but some will relax more if it's behind a closed door, you know your dogs. If you find that they are 'creating' whining whinging etc. then filled frozen Kongs or a chew are a good thing to give them before you leave them so they have something to do and so they think it's a good thing. Starting this ideally when you decide to get another puppy gives you plenty of time to iron out any creases and make it a habit before you and the dogs having the distraction of a puppy.

This is the perfect time to start some training on control around doorways and feed times if you don't do this usually. After all, I'm sure your current dog or dogs will need a little reminder of a few manners as we humans let things slip after a while.

Most multi-dog household fights occur around feeding time or around doorways that create frustration. This may be the door to the garden, the front door, in my case this would be the kitchen door where we all come and go from.

Training the dogs to wait or hang back when you open a door before being given a command or gesture to allow them through, or not as the case may be (you are leaving them in the room while you exit). This should be extended to the doors to go into the garden, doorways, and gateways when leaving the house for a walk, etc. this isn't as some people may think 'to show them who is boss' this is manners and bringing their arousal levels down around critical places that cause excitement. If you are training 'wait' and the dog will be released to go through the door with you or into the garden, regularly ask for a sit or similar when they have gone through the door before letting them go or before progressing onto the next doorway gate/carrying on with your walk. Practicing control both sides of each door or barrier removes the yank on the lead or the hoolie once they are through the door (this is particularly useful for dogs who charge out and into the garden barking). Wait or asking your dogs to back up/reverse when you walk into the room or area they are in will also help with this.

Consistency is key here, this needs to be EVERY time you walk through the door, so it becomes a habit, second nature to both them and us. A crowded doorway with multiple dogs jumping around on top of each other creates real potential for fights.

Depending what level you have trained your dogs to previous to this if you have multiple dogs already you may need to start by teaching each dog individually to do this before adding another and practicing and so on until you can do it with the whole pack together.

Most of these exercises are to do with bringing down frustration levels. If someone walked into my house with my favourite cake and waved it under my nose then said no you can't have it….I would get frustrated and eventually snap or shout at them "gimme the CAKE" (maybe I need more training? Can you tell I love cake?). If however the same person walked in and said if you wait nicely for a few seconds, you can have some cake I would be more likely to be patient, a more pleasant situation all around.

16
Introductions

Bringing puppy home

Make sure all existing family dogs have had a good walk before you return home with the puppy. Plenty of chews or frozen filled Kongs ready. Keep your existing dogs in another room (ideally one they are used to relaxing in and provide new Kongs or chews at this point). Puppy will likely need to toilet when you get out of the car, so straight to the garden and praise when they have performed. Bring them into the house, offer them a drink, the stress of travelling will have made them thirsty. They may not drink straight away, but at least they know where to find water for later. Let them explore in their own time – the prime opportunity for you to make yourself a drink and sit down while watching them from a distance. Once they have explored without the other dogs being there and depending on the time of day they may need feeding, feed them in their pen or area they will be expected to sleep in, etc. toilet trip outside again and then place them in their pen. Ideally, at this point, they will rest for a while.

All the excitement of a new home and traveling will have tired them out. If they cry for a short while, please ignore them, if however they scream and panic for longer than a few minutes take them out to toilet again and repeat. Once the puppy is asleep, this is a great time to let your adult dogs out for a wee, or someone (if you do not live alone) could maybe walk them or play with them in the garden). I must stress at this point the dogs should not be allowed anywhere near the puppy pen - even in passing, maybe to get to the garden, etc. This is to ensure the puppy feels comfortable and ideally stays asleep. Put adult dogs away again, with more chews.

Once the puppy has woken up, toilet trip, let them explore again and maybe have a play session with them with a toy. If you have cats, this would be the ideal time to let them meet, if the cats want to of course. Same applies to any other animals such as rabbits, birds, small caged animals. Short interactions with lots of rewards for the puppy. After another toilet trip and sleep for puppy it's time to introduce the dogs. This is where your barrier training pays off. Ideally a moveable barrier or a baby gate that pup and dogs can see through (but not so the puppy can squeeze through the bars).

Before we continue, I cannot express how important getting the introductions right and taking it at each dogs pace is. This is the key to success. We humans make snap decisions within the first few minutes of meeting other people on if we like them or not, sometimes consciously sometimes its subconsciously but it will shape how we interact with this person from then on. The same applies to dogs, though they seem to make decisions in a matter of seconds rather than minutes. We want the dogs to like each other rather than tolerate. This makes for a happier household for years to come.

Another reminder on how important the exercises pre-puppy are, as most if not all will be invaluable in this first day with the new puppy and moving forward.

There are a few things to consider here. If you have an impulsive, act first ask questions later type dog, or an over-friendly dog, a lead may be needed for initial interactions.
Treats at the ready for both pup and adult dog (maybe a glass of wine available for you to celebrate after). I try not to do this in a doorway due to doorway frustration issues, but this may be your only option (again why control around doors will really help).

If possible the first dog (if you have more than one) to meet puppy should be the calmest, ideally smallest, and if you have the same breed as puppy then same breed (puppy will recognize and be comfortable with its own breed from its mother and possibly other dogs at the breeder's property). This is in an ideal world, and let's face it this rarely happens! The priority here above all else is the calmest most laid back dog.

Both dog and puppy should have plenty of space to move back away from the barrier if they choose to. Puppy should be in the area it has been allowed to explore and ideally not its pen, but not a big issue if it is (just consider how much space it has to get away if it wants to, also only give adult dog access to one side of the pen, so pup doesn't feel trapped). Alternatively, if you can divide your garden this could be an option too (dry, non-windy weather needed for puppies comfort and confidence).

If you have more than one adult dog, only introduce one dog to the puppy at a time, do not over face and overwhelm them with multiple dogs in the first instance, this is often a recipe for disaster, creating a fear of dogs within the puppy.

Have treats in your hand when letting the other dog into the room where interactions with the puppy/barrier will take place, so they are interested in you and the treats to avoid them rushing straight for the barrier/pup.

You should stay on the side of the adult dog at all times to manage their behavior.

I captured all first interactions for my own study and use for clients after on video. This may be useful to trainers reading this. If you would like to see the first interactions between my adult five and Ripple get in touch and I will provide you with the link to view them.

Interactions should be kept to 2-3 minutes each

A lot of this chapter, well actually the whole book is meant as a guide and each dog and puppy is different so even shorter interactions may be needed for a nervous puppy or a highly excitable dog.

If puppy and dog sniff between bars I only let this happen for around 5 seconds before calling the adult dog away and rewarding them before allowing them to return.
If at this point the puppy is excited, relaxed, happy, interested and adult dog is calm and or focused on me, I may open the barrier to allow both dogs access to each other but will remove the adult dog if any play is attempted, or pushy bolshy behaviour, it goes without saying if there has been any growling or barking from either dog I remove the adult dog instantly. And repeat the barrier meeting later.

If however puppy is scared and runs away from the barrier/adult dog, let them move away, do not try to coax them closer. Ask your adult dog to sit or down facing away from the barrier, you may need a lot of treats for this, depending on how excited/interested your dog is about the new puppy. By turning them away this is offering a calming signal to the puppy who will be more likely to approach the barrier again to get a closer look/smell. When the puppy does this verbally praise them, maybe throw a treat over the barrier for them, so the treat goes behind the puppy who will then move away from the barrier to get the treat. If the puppy gets the treat, then approaches the barrier again this is a positive sign that they are becoming more relaxed and inquisitive. I would repeat this a few times before allowing the adult dog to turn around to face the puppy through the barrier calmly. Repeat the above stages appropriately depending on the puppy's reaction to being confronted again with the adult dog.

To give you an idea of timescales, we arrived home with Ripple around 1 pm and introductions started around 4.30 pm. All introductions were done within 15/20 minutes which were then followed by feeding my adult dogs (one day of lots of chews/treats and being fed as normal will not make your dog fat). Two of my five adult dogs were on lead for the barrier interactions and Ripple was confident and wanted to interact with each dog.

Once the adult dogs have been out to toilet post feeding, a puppy will also need to toilet in this time so planning this is key too for successful housetraining. Again puppy needs to toilet without the presence of the other dogs.

If all has gone well up to this point then barrier introductions with multiple dogs (ideally no more than two adults at a time) progressing to without the barrier for a couple of minutes each time.

If all hasn't gone so well up to this point then, don't panic, some more management needs to be put into place, plus a little patience. You may need to revisit this routine the next day or a few hours later. Or both until you have positive body language from both puppy and adult dogs. Keep dogs separate still, but ensure both puppy and adults have enough quality time with you and the human family. It will come! No point rushing it only to regret it later. A few days of being separated is not going to harm them, and in fact, it gives you more time to bond with puppy individually so they settle and trust you and your decisions which then will help each introduction attempt.

A wagging tail is not always a happy tail!

This can differ breed to breed, but I will use a Labrador as an example – mid-level (tail in a straight line out from the back, level with the dogs topline) steady wag is a happy dog, low or high positioning of tail with short stiff wags can be arousal, uncertainty or potential threat. Puppies use these methods of body language too so read both parties.
A great book about dog body language and posturing is Roger Abrantes – 'Dog Language'. It has plenty of clear diagrams too.

Once you have introduced each dog successfully (and without the barrier and at least in twos), the puppy can be in its pen, and the other dogs are milling around the outside of the pen at their leisure.

Puppy is only ever loose with the adult dogs when you can watch like a hawk!

Potential dangers here are:

Sharp puppy teeth biting at adult dogs; distract puppy and dog with treats scattered on the floor or with toys (i.e., don't do that, do this instead), before adult dog 'tells puppy off'.

Large adult dogs standing, sitting, lying on the puppy by accident – puppy skeletons are like jelly, very soft and this kind of incident can do a lot of damage to pup both mentally and physically. If you have a sizeable bouncy dog, for the first few days it may be best to keep them on lead with you when the puppy is loose to avoid this happening.

Adult dogs becoming possessive or guarding toys/chews/resting areas such as beds – now you should have minimized the risk of this by doing all the exercises stated in a previous chapter, but if this happens either remove said toys or treats (move all dogs away or into another room before removing the item, do not just grab toy/chew).

Sounds like hard work!

The first 24-72 hours are always the hardest and should be planned carefully, with other human members of the household on board and aware of the plan.

17
Days 1-7: this is hard work

Remember that puppy will want and need to sleep a lot if not most of the time in the first week that you bring them home. Make the most of it. This phase is gone before you know it!

Ripple example for our first 48 hours:

Day 1

After walking our adult dogs, we arrived at the breeder's house (20 minutes away) at 10 am, leave at 11 am and stop off on the way home to meet my in-laws, travelled on my lap (10 minutes) with blanket smelling of littermates and snuggle pup (fake heartbeat). No whining or crying while travelling, relaxed, happy to be held.

Two wees at in-laws in the garden,
Lots of cuddles and exploring
Two periods of sleep while there.
One visit to the garden and no wee
Home around 1 pm after letting adult dogs out to toilet they are shut away with frozen Kongs to let Ripple acclimatise.
Feed in pen, shut in pen and ignored for a short period
Two wees in garden
Two periods of sleep
3 pm adult dogs toilet/garden access for a short period without coming into contact with Ripple.

Exposure to the cat, household noises (Hoover, dishwasher, coffee machine, etc.)

Two more wees in garden

One more sleep

Introductions to the dogs, individually 4.30 - 5 pm

Chew bones all around 5.05 pm

Sleep at 5.20 pm

6 pm awake and wee

10 min play, 5 min play, and Fern second introduction

6 pm sleep in my arms

8 pm feed and wee

Adult dogs are milling around while Ripple is in pen and they are in the same room.

Sleep

10.30 pm awake, quick play session

Outside but no toilet 10.45 pm

Tried to play, too tired put in pen 11.10 pm with a few treats in a Kong

Settled/asleep 11.40 pm

3.30 am wee

Notes - shivering when outside, and not getting warm very quickly when returned indoors. Using   microwaveable heat pad in the pen and plan to use in a soft crate when traveling.

No poo, slightly worried but bright in herself, not dehydrated, hope she will do one in the night or the morning, if not - call the breeder and visit vet.

Day 2

7 am wee and feed

7.15 am first poo (never been so happy to see a puppy poo!)

Snooze on the sofa on me till 8 am

Play with toy

8.40 am asleep on lap

9.30 am wee

Then in pen with a hoof chew to settle

11 am poo and wee

12 pm feed and wee

Sleep at Mark's feet, with other dogs loose around her

12.45 pm wee

Feet trim nail clip fuss

Potter round with others supervised

1.20 pm pen to relax
2.20 pm wee
Relax with Mark on the sofa
3.20 pm out for wee and poo
Take pup to horse livery yard, first time in the crate on own in the car, fine. Left her in there to catch Billy in the field (pony) 10-15 min left in car and fine/settled/quiet (left her in there mainly to stay warm). Met Billy, and two people at the yard, home 4.30 pm
A visitor came to stay for the night, Alan. Introduced Fern (and others) while Ripple was in the car, so she was not subjected to Fern's barking (this is the management bit).
4.35 pm wee in the garden then meet Alan.
Feed then sleep in the pen
Out for wee but didn't 6 pm
To pub on Alan's lap in car 6.30 pm
Asleep in the soft crate at the pub
7 pm wee in the pub garden
Cuddled by two staff at the pub, plus one customer and Alan, calm taking it all in.
Home 8.15 pm wee and feed
Play in pen on own
10.00- 11.15 pm on Mark's lap,
11.45 pm wee and poo
Play on own and with Mark
12.40 am outside but no wee
12.45 am placed in the pen, settled and asleep within 5 min.
Out for wee at 3.30 am - we wouldn't usually stay up till this time, but Alan and I were up chatting.

Notes - settles well in the soft crate, especially with the heat.
Likes to sleep when travelling.
Poos are now happening regularly so not worried.
Likes to watch what's going on
Fern is keeping distance, so not totally happy (to be expected) it will take time but making the best choice and keeping away if Ripple is running around.
All the other dogs happy and accepting.
Moss is actively looking for her if she is not in pen, in a calm way.
Likes to play tug, working on fetch
Happy to be carried in arms or in the soft crate.
Very affectionate and licky.

Having a puppy requires you to have eyes in the back of your head! If I cannot watch her, and I mean watch her every move, she is either on Marks lap, in her soft crate or in the pen where she is safe. This is for her safety, the other dogs' safety and for housetraining.
I am getting up in the middle of the night, not because she is waking me, in fact, the opposite. I set my alarm to wake me to take her out as she isn't physically able to hold it all night, this way it helps prevent her learning to toilet in the house (though there is a puppy pad in her crate as an emergency option). It also stops her screaming waking us up to take her out which then rewards the noise. Hopefully, I won't be doing this for more than a couple of weeks.

Note: I got up in the middle of the night for 11 nights, before she could hold it all night (approximately 7-8 hours).

Don't worry I won't be boring you with every single second of her life but the first 48 hours may be helpful when considering getting a puppy, what it entails, and to start on the right track it begins from the second they are in your care.

Make sure you have a few days clear for when the pup comes home, not everything will go to plan, but if you are there you can cope and adapt to what is needed. Keeping calm is crucial, pups absorb our energy and look to us for guidance if we are calm and collected it will set them up to be too.

Try your best to keep to your adult dogs' regular routines, i.e. when they eat, sleep, etc. You can add to this with more walks and chews etc. but as much as possible, please do not lessen their time and interactions with you.

This also helps the pup realise that although they are important, there are others that you will be distracted by and helps them learn how to cope with frustration.

I usually make sure any of my new dogs are not left alone in the house for the first three days, then start to build up short periods of isolations, 20 minutes, 30, an hour and so on and so forth. By the time they have been home for a week I have usually got to the point where I can confidently leave them for up to 2 hours in their pen and no other dogs in sight while we are out of the house. I always leave the puppy with something to do such as a frozen stuffed Kong and make sure all their needs are met before going to ensure they are tired, full and comfortable (not full of beans, a full bladder and hungry). Depending on whether you live alone or not, this may not be possible. You will have to leave the house to walk the dogs at some point. In cases like this, I would advise either taking pup on the walk (provided all the dogs are well behaved on a walk) in a carrier or pouch for the first three days or ask someone else to walk the dogs or puppy sit on those days.

18

The first 8 weeks: Socialisation, socialisation, socialisation...then the hormones start to appear

The optimum socialisation period is from 3-12 weeks, for some breeds, this can go on until 16 weeks. During this time the more, short positive experiences they can have with the big wide world the better. Different types of people, traffic, pushchairs, wheelchairs, horses, other species, weather, sounds, smells the better. The key thing to remember is short periods of exposure, positive (if they are not scared) and with plenty of opportunity to sleep/rest between new experiences. Socialisation to the world is the most important thing and should be prioritised above all else while in this age bracket, they can learn to sit and wait, etc. later. Correct socialisation can be the difference between a lifelong happy, well-rounded companion or an insecure or aggressive shaking wreck. After 12 weeks socialisation should continue, for months if not years but what pup learns in the initial window is the basis for everything else.

Around two weeks after the pup has come home, they will start to push the boundaries. This is the same for an adult rescue dog, a friend's dog staying or for a pup who is the only dog in the household. They have figured out what the rules are at this point and start to figure out how they might be able to get around them, be prepared for this and know that it is normal. The key is to stay calm and find ways that you can reinforce the rules, practice more waits at doorways, waits for food/treats, putting them down for jumping on the sofa when you have asked them not to for example.

Somewhere within this period, your older dogs will change towards your puppy, and they will be less forgiving and patient. This is what I describe as your puppy losing its 'puppy licence' the time has gone that older dogs will put up with everything the puppy throws at them. It's usually at around 16 weeks, the hormones start to kick in around this time, not usually to the extent that you will notice a change in behaviour from the puppy, but the older dogs sense this. Normally it's nothing more than your adult dogs sticking up for themselves and giving a low grumble or air snap if the pup is being too much. Of course, as long as you are supervising interactions and preventing play the effect at this time will be very minimal, but worth being mindful of all the same.

Usually, once pup has been home for six weeks, and I'm happy with interactions between dogs when they are together I feel comfortable enough to pop out to the toilet or answer the door for deliveries, without putting the pup in a separate area to the other dogs. If however there are still some 'teething' problems, i.e. adult dogs regularly growling or avoiding puppy I will not venture out of the room at all when the pup is loose with the adult dogs as I can't be confident of what will happen in even a brief absence.

When I introduced Jazz (Ripples grandma, Moss's Mum now sadly deceased) to Ziggy and Bella (Bella also deceased, RIP), I did not follow all of the rules in this book. I was still learning at that point. I remember it took a whole month for Ziggy to not growl at Jazz being in his immediate vicinity. Ziggy is a very easy going dog, friendly to everyone and everything but looking back now I can see my lack of intervention and management meant he felt overwhelmed at being around those little needle sharp teeth so much, despite him being just a year old when Jazz first came home (another no-no in the rule of four).

However after a month or so, Jazz and Ziggy became great buddies, Jazz was naturally of higher social position than Ziggy, and in most play between the two, Ziggy would end up worse off, but still went back for more. They ended up being over bonded as I didn't do enough with Jazz separately. When Jazz passed away Ziggy grieved for a very long time, certainly over a year before he had his little spark back. I guess the point I'm trying to make here is even the softest of dogs get fed up with puppies, so please, please for their sakes and yours keep up with strict management routines, spending more time with puppy individually than pup spends with your other dogs.

In these first weeks you will get tired, exhausted even. A puppy on its own is a lot of hard work, housetraining, training, playing, etc. You will be giving up more time than usual to spend with your pack because ideally, you should still be spending the same time as before with your established adult dog or dogs and then spending extra time with puppy doing all the puppy things. In effect, you will have no downtime, and this will affect your mood and energy levels.

It's very easy to give up on what I'm asking you to do at this stage because it's easier and because you need a break. When you get to this point, start by upping the chews and stuffed Kongs again so you can get some peace for a while, and if that's still not enough, please ask someone else for help, ask them to pup sit or to walk your adult dogs.

I understand it's so tempting to think/say oh well everyone is getting on well let's just let pup have free rein and make life easier......it may be more comfortable short term but long term you will end up paying the price.

Dogs and puppies are always learning, not just when we are training! They are always seeking information, does this work, if I do this does it pay? When I say pay, I don't mean with treats (although a dog that learns to steal food off the kitchen side certainly does get paid for that behaviour). 'If I run out into the garden and another dog chases me does that feel good?' for most pups and dogs the answer will be yes, practiced just a handful of times and it is a hard habit to break and often results in all the dogs charging into the garden barking because they think it's fun, and this is a problem.

A lot and I really mean a lot of blood sweat and often tears go into these first weeks, but are the basis for an easier happier life for the lifetime of your puppy. Keep calm and carry on!

A little note about feeding/weight of your pup during this time

A recent study has shown that puppies grow at the fastest rate up to 16 weeks and growth slows after this age, it seems to be a common thing for people to keep their puppies 'chubby' and while this makes sense with the speed that they grow it should only be under 16 weeks of age and within reason!

This study has now found that maintaining an 'ideal weight' (going on body score, rather than kilos, pounds and ounces) from 15/16 weeks is more beneficial to your puppy. In other words, this is when the metabolism starts to mature and will set the basis for its life. For example, a puppy who is kept slightly overweight at 16 weeks will always have a slightly slower metabolism and will be more prone to weight gain in adulthood and make it harder for you to get them to shed the pounds when needed. A pup at 16 weeks with a 'normal' body score is more likely to maintain the same body score throughout its life, and if it happens to gain weight, you will find it easier to get the pounds off.

19

4 months to 6 months; hormones and more hormones, growth, learning, and teething

Puppies are often still teething up to 6 months, so there may be points where your pup doesn't want to eat or stops picking up toys in its mouth because the gums are sore. Try not to worry and be mindful of what type of food you are feeding them (if it's hard kibble maybe try soaking it in boiled water and leaving to cool before feeding).

Your pup will still be finding its feet within the family and has all these changes in its body to contend with too. It is still very much a baby and still very impressionable. If you have adult dogs whose behaviour you don't want a pup to learn during this stage you still need to be sheltering from experiencing, watching or having the opportunity to join in with this unwanted behaviour.

Walks should still be separate from your adult dogs and continued socialisation exercises with different environments etc. are still very important.

By this stage I'm still not leaving pup and adult dogs alone together for more than five minutes, I'm still using the puppy pen and ensuring all adult dogs continue to be happy and content when in the company of pup.

It's still of great importance that you are taking the pup out on separate walks and outings, so they gain their own confidence and find their own little feet in the world.

The odd outing with one or two of your best behaved older dogs isn't going to hurt as long as you are concentrating on the pup and gaining pup's attention despite being around other family members on a walk or outing. When I say the odd outing, I mean maybe one outing out of 10, or even 20.

Group outings should not be the norm until after 12 months of age

This will be hard to maintain. Life gets busy, pup seems to be doing well, time is of the essence, and stress levels seem to creep up when life doesn't go to plan. If life is getting stressful and you are finding it hard to take the time to take pup out separately, you are very unlikely to be in the 'training mind frame' when you do take pup out with the adult dogs. It only takes a couple of walks of the pup thinking 'ooh it's fun to chase my brother/sister and bark/yell/pounce on them when they are excited' and this is a tough habit to break….not a good formula for stress free walks in future. When you are finding yourself getting to this point, there are other solutions!
Take adult dog or dogs out on their regular walk, play with and train pup in the garden or the home. The puppy isn't going to lose out from the odd day of not going on a walk (yes, shoot me now, I said it! But it's true, and so much better than the alternative).

Just 3 x 3 minute training sessions a day is the quickest most effective way to teach not only new behaviours (this can be tricks, general control, training for competition, loose lead walking in the garden) but also the quickest way to tire them out. Mentally this is equivalent to an hours walk!

Exercise for your pup - how much is too much? Often less than you think

The very general rule and probably the easiest to remember is 'the 5 minute rule.'

Only walk your pup for 5 minutes for each month of life. For example, a 6 month old puppy should only be having 30 minutes exercise (5 minutes x 6 months = 30 minutes). This should be for all breeds up to

Labrador size up until 12 months of age, and for larger breeds such as Newfoundlands, Great Danes, St Bernards, etc. up to 2 years of age. Why? Because as I've said in previous chapters, puppy's bones and joints are still developing, they are very soft and can easily be damaged.

I have done it all wrong before, with Ziggy when he was a tiny pup, I took him out with my bigger, older dog Bella every day for an hour, Bella would chase a ball back and forth for the whole of the walk, and Ziggy would chase behind her. I did this from a young age (maybe 4/5 months old) and I remember taking him to the vet for something routine at around 8 or 9 months old and saying to the vet, 'I'm sure I'm over exercising this pup' (I was not working with dogs professionally then, and knew very little, other than I wanted the very best for my dogs and had limited knowledge). The vet responded with something like, 'oh he's a small dog, he will let you know when he's had enough, don't worry about it'. At age 18 months Ziggy was diagnosed with arthritic hips, and this was due to my naivety of over exercising him while he was still growing and maturing.

Ziggy isn't, never has and never will be the type of dog who will let me know when he's 'had enough' he would go all day if I let him, he's still a bouncy, happy chap at almost 13 years of age but when he does 'overdo it' he is stiff that evening or the next day. The five-minute rule is becoming more and more common knowledge which is great, but there is still the misconception that it only applies to big dogs. It refers to all sizes, as Ziggy and many others have proven.

Think about it in human terms. You would not ask a 5-year-old child to walk for 10 miles would you? Nor would you ask a 10-year-old child to carry a heavy load.

In dog agility you are not allowed to compete with your dog until they are 18 months of age, this is due to the wear and tear on their bodies when jumping/landing, twisting and turning through weaves and doing a tight turn to the next piece of equipment. In most other dog sports there is a minimum age limit to compete and another to move up a level too. Again due to their bodies maturing, and to help prevent damage.

The five-minute rule is great, an even better guide to work from is the Puppy Culture puppy exercise guide which you can buy online or view on google images. It's very specific with types of exercise and size of dog and age of the dog.

Other things to consider while the pup is still growing are things like how often they are jumping off furniture, if you are allowing them to jump in and out of vehicles, playing with other dogs (not just your own family of dogs) and going up and down stairs. All of these things have an impact on their joints and should be kept to an absolute minimum while young to ensure long-lasting health in their adult life.

During this phase, there is nothing wrong with occasionally meeting up with friends and their adult dogs (provided that they are good role models for the pup of course) and going for a short stroll or meeting at a cafe or pub or going around to their house for a catch-up. This teaches the puppy that other dogs are ok too, but putting a lot of importance on not doing this where the other dog is still young and very playful.

One of the biggest problems I see with dogs from multi-dog households is when the youngest is barking/lunging/pulling, frustrated and wants to get to other dogs all the time. This is usually because they spend 90% of their lives with free access to the other dogs in the household and don't understand why they can't 'go and say hi' to every other dog it sees.

Meeting up with friends role model dogs like the ones described previously will reduce the risk of your pup becoming a 'frustrated greeter', alongside teaching them to ignore the presence of other dogs unless you say otherwise.

More importance should be put on passing dogs on walks calmly. The pup does not get to meet every dog it sees, and it gets a reward for coming past dogs or seeing dogs at a distance and not pulling toward them. A reward can be a fuss, treat or a play session in this instance, depending on what's appropriate/easiest for you at the time. Try not to only rely on a stroke or fuss as a reward for this as will not be enough 'wages/payment' to pup in some instances and will lead to them eventually becoming the frustrated greeter. For example - the dog at a distance, puppy responds to you calling its name easily = fuss/good dog. Dog a little closer, pup responds to you or ignores dog completely = treat or play. Dogs are all about distance…the closer something is, the harder it is to ignore…so pay your pup accordingly.

Also, it's worth remembering that there will be instances your pup cannot possibly listen or respond to you….this is usually because the other dog is simply too close and too interesting. In these instances, stay calm and relaxed and simply move pup further away to a distance where it can respond to you and be rewarded. Try not to keep calling pup's name, talking or shouting at it when it is in the frenzied state of wanting to get to the other dog, your energy is being fed to pup and it will react in a negative way to this (i.e. I would definitely rather be with my own kind right now than with this unstable, frustrated, angry human). Not only that but the more times you call pup's name, and it ignores you the more it learns that ignoring you is an option and it can be repeated next time. Just move away with the puppy, staying quiet and reward when the pup is more relaxed and can respond.

20

6 months and beyond; it's not over yet

Sexual maturity (not mental nor physical) is reached during this stage. For females, sexual maturity comes with their first season and with males its harder to put your finger on other than their testing and testosterone-fueled behaviour, though it's after around 10 months for medium to large breeds (Springer Spaniels to Labradors, etc.). This is often younger for smaller breeds, say 7/8 months for my main breed, Miniature Dachshunds or around 12-14 months for giant breeds such as Great Danes. Your adult dogs will know when the pup is reaching sexual maturity and will act differently around them.

This is a rite of passage in many ways for your pup, and often I see the adult dogs be more forceful in their reprimands toward the puppy. Just like when a teenage human is pushing boundaries, and the parents come down hard on them. This usually passes provided you have picked the right mix of social positions, and the pup is still left entire - not neutered or spayed at this point.

If however, the mix is wrong, this is usually the start of the end of the happy pack. This is another reason why I'm all for management and playing it cool with the dogs having time together, the more focused on you and or humans they are the less they will be bothered by the other dogs and or bother the other dogs which are likely to create conflict between them.

Often the owners of pups will have been led to believe around this age (6-8 months) is the best time to have their puppy neutered or spayed. Or they get frustrated with the hormone-fueled behaviour particularly in male dogs and get them 'fixed' with the belief not only is it the best thing for their dog but it is also likely to make the annoying behaviours lessen or stop completely. Unfortunately, this is rarely the case. I am not anti-spay/neuter, nor am I pro. My own experiences both professionally and from what my dogs tell me (aside from the complicated considerations for a multi-dog household) that having them 'fixed' at this age, lessens their ability to grow up mentally. We wouldn't do it to a teenage boy or girl so why would we do it to a dog? Neutering early (i.e., before the body has fully grown and matured) in male dogs is proven to make them grow taller and can cause bone and joint issues in the future. With female dogs, you are removing the hormones that keep them calm, and while in both sexes it takes 12 weeks for the hormones to dissipate totally, and usually people see an improvement during this period. The issues that they had hoped to fix usually return after this period of adjustment. Now this isn't the case for all, and yes there are benefits to spay and neuter for which I'm sure you have heard from your vet. But if you can wait just another 6-12 months it will make little to no difference to their chances of cancer, and you will end up with a more rounded, mature adult dog at the end of it. Do some research, particularly for your breed (or the mix of breeds if applicable). Each breed is different, and most breed clubs will have guidelines and advice sheets on this subject. The Dachshund breed council are now recommending if and only if you would like to get your dog spayed or neutered its best to do it once they are over 2 years (considering this is a small, fast maturing breed, it wasn't what I was expecting) neutering younger can increase their chances of back problems.

In some breeds such as the Golden Retriever and Rottweiler it's been found that neutering male dogs is detrimental and is likely to cause osteoporosis. Every dog is different, and every breed is different, and also your mix of dogs, so a lot to consider here.

It's worth remembering with male dogs once their hormones have peaked, things start to get easier, it's not going to be like that forever! Just sit tight, keep calm and breathe!
Female dogs often calm down in their behaviour after their first season, but then start to push boundaries, almost become manipulative in a very sneaky, subtle way - again sit tight and keep calm, it will get easier.

Secondary fear period:

This is something which you may notice or you may not, but it's
certainly worth keeping an eye out for. For large breeds such as
German Shepherds, this is usually around 7 months of age, younger for
smaller breeds and older for larger. This is a period in which your dog
may 'spook' or become fearful of sights and sounds that they have
previously been okay with. This usually passes fairly quickly.
Sometimes after a couple of days in other cases, it can be 2-3 weeks.
During this time it's important that your pup isn't exposed to things that
could make him very fearful. The odd spook is fine but if they have a
bad experience such as a dog attacking them during this time it is
something that will stay with them for months and often years ahead.
This stage is normal as part of your pup's development. You may find
they become a little barkier at general things during this period, in
which case it's essential to manage the amount that they can practice
barking at things that can trigger this behaviour during this period.

7-11 months is the hardest stage of having a pup, even harder when you
have multiple dogs. This is when you will start to see any behaviour
passed on from your adult dogs, and I don't mean the good ones! Pup
will be pushy, have little to no concentration, have days where it will
feign deafness, and you will question whether you did ever teach them
to sit, wait, or anything for that matter. Training wise…more patience
needed. Yes, even more than before. Back to basics with training and
making everything as easy as possible for them. For example, if they
could previously do a one minute stay and now can barely do 30
seconds, just ask for 20 seconds for a few repetitions before gradually
building up to a minute in small increments. Don't be stingy or tight
with your rewards, pay your dog well and he/she will want to repeat it
and even try harder the next time!

Recall or coming when called when off lead usually starts to be
affected during this stage, go somewhere else, hide from your dog,
make it fun, take better smellier treats for coming back, don't let them
have as much off lead exercise as before so you can concentrate on
increasing their response to the recall command while they are off lead.

Your pup or adolescent is still learning (and quite obviously testing you
and the boundaries) at this age which is why I would advise against
them being walked with the rest of the pack or the adult dog in the
house. You need to concentrate on giving them a good grounding of

training more at this stage than at any other, and with their limited concentration you need to use this for you rather than let them concentrate on 'joining in with the others'.

Neural pruning

This happens around 10 - 12 months for small to medium dogs and 12-18 months for large breeds, 18-24 months for giant breeds.

It's your pup's brain filtering out what is important information and what's not, linked to this is the secondary fear period as described above. Just like your computer doing a defrag, or emptying the trash folder. It's your pups brain deciding what or who is safe and reliable in its world, what behaviours 'pay' (this can be a self-reward such as stealing food off the side or that they feel good when they chase or play with other dogs or it can be sitting and waiting for his food gets him a big reward- his meal at the end of it) and what behaviours don't pay. If you have ignored jumping up on you and not given eye contact, verbal commands or touched them (which can all be perceived as rewards) consistently, your dog will deem this behaviour as a waste of energy and cease to repeat it. The brain is also filtering out and in what 'the pack does,' and this is where all your hard work of protecting them from unwanted behaviours of other dog family members starts to pay off. This doesn't mean once they have their first birthday they can do what they like, but it does mean you can begin to relax things and move forward as a whole pack rather than a pack plus a puppy.

Considering the size of your pup and what approximate age they should have completed neural pruning you can then start to work on 'pack walks' consistently, build it up gradually and don't forget that even at this age your youngster will still be learning all the time.

Following my advice and guidelines up to this point will have given you an excellent basis for an easier more manageable pack, and given your young dog its independence and confidence as an individual that will never have to worry about being left alone, and will look to you for guidance more than its fellow pack members. A massive pat on the back to you at this point. The journey to this stage hasn't been an easy one, and I'm sure many friends and family have mocked you for it, but at the end of the day, you can relax in the knowledge you have done the most you possibly could for a more comfortable life as part of a multi-dog household.

WELL DONE

.

21
Older dogs, pack issues when they are aging and grief

When older dogs start to deteriorate in physical or mental health, often the higher ranking pack members will appear to either ignore them (as if they don't exist) or they appear to start picking on them, worst case is when the older dog begins to be physically attacked by the others.

This is going to sound harsh, but I promise you it is true and this is a common thing that I am called out to help with. In a sense, the older dog is no longer a valuable and useful member of the pack and as such is being pushed out or outlawed by the others.

This said, always have the older dog vet checked if you see changes in how the other dogs interact with him or her. Even if you do not detect any issues in your older dog, quite often it can be an underlying health issue that medication may help (and therefore extend the time you have a balanced and happy group of dogs).

In cases where it's just two dogs in the household, one older one younger; when the older one passes away even though the two dogs may not have appeared to have interacted for months or maybe a couple of years, the younger dog will still grieve for the loss of its canine companion.

If you have a Leader, Enforcer or Peacekeeper who is elderly, and you do not have a dog who can 'take over' in that role, there will be some shifts within the pack, a transition period. This is never easy, particularly if you have a pack of more than three dogs. Don't forget, yes of course, dogs can and will take on an associated character when needed, but this is usually only the immediate characters above or below (except for the specialist roles). What I'm trying to say is don't expect an Onlooker character to become anything other than a Follower, just like it's not advisable to expect an Enforcer to become a Follower. A dog having to take a big jump into another character is all too often too much pressure, they will attempt to fill the gap but will be stressed, and it will not come naturally.

I'll say again if you have a pack full of Followers, other than the dogs grieving over a dog who has passed over, you are unlikely to see any issues with them trying to fill the position nor see them 'test' the elderly dog when it is still on this plane.

Dogs just like us go through a grieving process. This isn't just about losing their security if you have lost an Enforcer, it's also that they have lost what could be their favourite companion.

I remember when I lost Jazz (Moss's Mum) so unexpectedly, Ziggy who had a close bond with her was not the same for over a year after. Seven years on and I know he is still not the same dog he was (discounting him aging etc.), he is happy and has bonded with the more recent additions. He hasn't managed to bond quite as close as he did to Jazz, considering he is a reasonably lower ranking dog he hasn't managed to get that security in such a close bond again which I believe he benefitted greatly from when Jazz was around (even if she did push him around quite a bit, he actively sought her attention and company). The things to remember here are Ziggy and Jazz barely had 12 months between them, and I had not done all the work individually when Jazz was young (or not to the extent I should have), so they were borderline over bonded to each other.

I also know that when we lose Merlin, Moss will feel his loss the most. A bond was struck between them when Moss was just 5 or 6 weeks of age. They don't play, but they sleep and lie together at any and every opportunity, this is more Moss's choice than Merlin's so he will really miss his big black cuddle pillow.

Sometimes when our older dogs are singled out by the others, it's merely the safest for all concerned to keep the older dog separate from the rest of the pack. So your older dog can enjoy some peace, and it takes the strain off you and the other dogs too. Although this isn't ideal nor easy to put in place it is the safest option, and because of their older years, it won't be for an extended period. The advantage of doing this is that the younger dogs will often grieve less when the older dog passes as you have staggered the process.

If you decide that the time has come for your older dog to be helped on his way over the rainbow bridge, the best way to do this where possible is to call the vet out to your home, after euthanasia, let the dogs in to sniff the body individually, this will help them comprehend the permanent loss of their companion. If this isn't possible, rubbing a towel or blanket over the body of the deceased and bringing home for the dogs to smell would be a close second.

When we lose a dog it's so very hard on us too, all the years we have spent with a beautiful soul, and now they are gone. We need to grieve, and our emotions will, of course, be picked up on by our dogs, and that's ok.

We all grieve in different ways. Some people swear never to have another (some will eventually and some won't) some go out and get another dog straight away others wait and get one in time....I've done or said all of these. It's not about what others think, it's about what feels right for you and your remaining dogs at the time, just remember if you are introducing a new pup in quick succession after losing one, your pack may not be as welcoming as they would be if they were not grieving, so extra work with integration may be needed.

Conclusion

A reminder to stick to the plan! On your head be it if you skip some steps.

In essence

Make sure your new dog has its own identity as an individual, has experienced many things with you and without the rest of the pack, and don't get lazy with it......you are looking at months of this to enjoy years and years of reaping the benefits.

Your new dog/puppy should be better or the best behaved of your gang, because of the above. If you don't do the work, they will end up the worst and drag the rest of the gang down with it.

Do you want wild dogs?

Do you want to have a happier and easier life in future for the sake of a few month's hard work?

Is it worth it....YES it really is worth it!

Do you want to be in a position where your dogs are fighting to the death, either with each other or other dogs on walks? No? Follow the blinking plan then.

A solution to when your friends make comments such as 'oh mine were fine', 'oh you're overthinking it', 'oh stop being a spoil sport', calling you the fun police, etc.? Buy them this book, you never know they may put some into practice with their established multi-dog household.. And realise all those little things that bug them are their own doing and tell them you have to live with the dogs and although it may have worked for them not putting the work in, you're not prepared to risk it.

Feeling guilty about shutting the older dogs out sometimes? Or take the new pup out and not the others? This is often short-term (though it is something I practice throughout their lives).
Life sucks sometimes, and that is an invaluable lesson for both dogs and humans.

'Short-term frustration for long-term relaxation'.

Final notes

There are exceptions to every rule, even I don't know everything!

We are all human, we are complex, and dogs are infinitely complex too, but I hope by reading this book that you have gained some insight and food for thought for if you do decide to add another dog to your household and how you will do it when you do.

My dogs are far from perfect, but they are happy and manageable. I never wanted robots!

If you have enjoyed reading this, please drop me a quick email to sarah@houndhelpers.co.uk and I will add you to our mailing list with regular free training tips and offers. I am currently working on an online puppy training course featuring Ripple (she's on the cover of this book). Plus a multi-dog house hold training course which I will be launching through my mailing lists.

There are also some great resources and videos on our Facebook page - Hound Helpers Ltd including the videos of initial introductions to the rest of the family with Ripple.

Thank you for reading and good luck!

Here are some resources I would recommend -

Dog Language by R Abrantes - a tremendous pictorial book on dog language & postures

The Perfect Puppy by Gwen Bailey - Puppy raising/training book

Puppy Culture - DVD Boxset by Jane Killion, fantastic puppy protocols from birth to 12weeks

https://www.kachinacanine.com/ - Dr Isla Fishburn for more information on Functional Characters

www.doglaw.co.uk – Trevor Cooper Dog Law Solicitor for help on all things regarding the Law with dogs in the UK

www.mykc.org.uk is a wonderful tool to use to check pedigrees, to check if your pup has been registered and of any health tests of the parents. You only need to ask for the bitch/mother of pup's registered name (as long as she is registered with the UK Kennel Club) for you to check more details through this website.

ABOUT THE AUTHOR

A qualified dog training instructor specialising in multi-dog households, reactive/barky dogs, and puppy training. A Kennel Club Accredited Instructor in companion dog training and KC Rally. QIDTI – qualified international dog training instructor. Sarah has been professionally training dogs for eight years. Her company Hound Helpers Ltd was launched in 2007, which has helped thousands of dogs over that time.

She is based between Evesham and Pershore in Worcestershire but is proud of her Yorkshire roots. She enjoys spending her free time competing in KC Rally and Obreedience with her Dachshunds, doing various horse sports and activities including competitive carriage driving with her Fell Pony, Billy.

26863498R00076

Printed in Great Britain
by Amazon